GREAT
NAVAL
BATTLES

GREAT NAVAL BATTLES

FROM MEDIEVAL WARS TO THE PRESENT DAY

HELEN DOE

This edition published in 2022 by Arcturus Publishing Limited
26/27 Bickels Yard, 151–153 Bermondsey Street,
London SE1 3HA

AD008798UK

Printed in the UK

MIX
Paper from
responsible sources
FSC® C171272

CONTENTS

CONTENTS

INTRODUCTION

An examination of naval battles over the centuries shows the great changes that came with new technology and battle tactics, although many factors remained the same, such as clear leadership skills. Early medieval fleets were made up of a random collection of merchant ships to carry troops, but by the twentieth century the vast and powerful aircraft carrier became the symbol of international power. Weaponry evolved from galley battering rams, to archers in ship forecastles, gunnery platforms, bomb vessels, to the great ironclads and nuclear submarines. The introduction of the three-masted ship brought greater manoeuvrability, the introduction of iron and steam revolutionized naval warfare by freeing warships from the fickle wind, while aircraft launched from carriers demanded a new way of thinking about seapower.

Making a selection of great naval battles is challenging. Numbers alone do not define a great battle, and a relatively small event can have a lasting impact, such as the Battle of Flamborough Head in 1779. The single ship duels of the War of 1812 were highly effective, while the battles of grand fleets were often confused. Not all great battles were clearly decisive; Jutland, for instance, is still causing much historical debate. Nor were battles purely fought by navies: the Battle of Pulo Aura in 1804 saw the French Navy losing a fight with a fleet of merchant ships. And not all battles were between officially warring foes, such as the confused Battle of Navarino in 1827, the last battle fought by sailing ships, or the Battle of Goodwin Sands that preceded the First Anglo Dutch War in 1652. Some engagements, such as the Battle of Chesapeake Bay in 1781, or the six-month Guadalcanal campaign in the Pacific during World War II, had far reaching consequences, which cannot be said for other battles. Good information on battles can be problematic, especially if the victorious nation writes the history. If an account of a battle is written by the commanding officer, he will naturally look to justify his decisions. The personal reminiscences and witness accounts of 'lesser' figures such as ordinary sailors and civilians are often overlooked but can add much to the picture. Timing is an issue; memories are fallible and an account written some years later can be unreliable. By the eighteenth century, newspapers were in use and although bias, misinformation and censorship can blur the picture, they provided vivid accounts to thrill the contemporary reader.

From a hastily assembled fleet of merchant vessels in the medieval period, over time the naval service developed. This was noticeable during the seventeenth century as the two great mercantile nations of the day, the English and the Dutch, gradually formed professional navies with all the necessary support and administration functions. Professional navies have been involved in the great struggles for world mastery from the French Revolutionary and Napoleonic wars to World Wars I and II. After the great arms race of the building of dreadnoughts before World War I, another decisive Trafalgar was anticipated, but navies proved less effective in that conflict. Airpower was the big influence from 1919 and World War II saw the importance and value of the aircraft carrier, while submarines brought another new dimension to the war at sea.

The great leaders shine through these battle accounts, but so too do the less well known heroes, men and even women, who fought at sea. Comparing great commanders is difficult, as each had to manage very different and complex scenarios, such as technology. In historian Paul Kennedy's neat summary: 'Nelson would have been at home on board a flagship of 150 years before but Jellicoe and Nimitz would have been lost on a ship of 100 years earlier.'

BATTLE OF SANDWICH

1217

*The Plantagenets were once proud rulers of territory
on either side of the English Channel and claimed
both the French and the English crowns. In the early
thirteenth century, however, the Channel was a wide
moat dividing the two warring nations. King John
of England had lost almost all of his lands in France
to a resurgent Philip II, and between 1203 and
1204 Philip expanded his kingdom and conquered
Normandy and Maine. With full access now to
the coast, the French carried out raids across the
Channel, many of them led by a pirate from Sark in
the Channel Islands who had the colourful name of
Eustace the Monk. This conflict led to the first battle
known to be fought at sea under sail.*

King John continued to lead campaigns to regain his lost territory with limited success, culminating in a major loss to the French at Bouvines in 1214. In England, the heavy taxation to pay for these wars was causing civil unrest and the French sought to profit from the unsettled situation. With encouragement from many English barons, Louis, heir to King Philip, landed at Thanet and succeeded in occupying great swathes of the southern part of England, including London. King John died in October 1216 and his heir, now proclaimed King Henry

II, was only nine years old. Fortunately for England the Regent was William Marshall, a man of very considerable experience. Under his leadership the tide began to turn against the French forces in southern England, although Prince Louis still had London. In order to retain his control Louis needed major reinforcements from France. To help with the French siege of Dover his wife, Blanche of Castile, raised funds for a fleet to transport several hundred knights, their horses, crossbow men and infantry, together with supplies, money and a trebuchet (a massive catapult).

Marshall needed to stop these reinforcements reaching Prince Louis so he headed for the Cinque Ports. These were a confederation of southern ports including Hastings, New Romney, Hythe, Dover and Sandwich that dated back to the previous century and they had considerable maritime power. Their loyalty had been tested by the arrival of the French but William Marshall offered to restore their privileges and, with the promise of a profitable share in the forthcoming attack on the French fleet, regained their support. By 19 August, William Marshall was in Romney and he had the benefit of access to an impressive fleet courtesy of the late King John. (By 1212, at a time when the majority of ships were privately owned, King John kept at least 50 royal galleys at Portsmouth and is seen by some as the father of the English navy.)

On 20 August, the French left Calais aiming for the Thames Estuary, but poor weather forced them to return. They finally set out four days later. According to French records, the French fleet comprised around 80 ships. Ten of them were large fighting ships transporting the knights and sergeants, while the rest were carrying supplies. Eustace the Monk was in his flagship, which was heavily laden, as its cargo included the warhorses and the siege engine. The English numbers vary in the records between a fleet of 40 and a fleet of 22 ships. There were probably at least 16 armed vessels, with several support ships and a combination of galleys and ships. While the numbers look significantly different, the French ships were very heavily laden and low in the water, while the English ships were smaller, lighter and were purely attack vessels.

Eustace, the French commander, watched as the English squadron, led by Hubert de Burgh, sailed from Kent and passed astern of them. Battles at sea were rare and Eustace thought they were planning to head towards Calais in order to attack that port. In fact, de Burgh was simply using the advantage of the wind and once they were astern of the French fleet they attacked. Ship engagements at sea were normally stationary and involved grappling or ramming. Once within range, crossbows and javelins could then be used. But with the wind behind them the English had the advantage of another weapon. They threw pots of quicklime at the enemy vessels, which broke on the ships in clouds and blinded the men on board. The hand-to-hand fighting was brutal, breaking limbs and smashing heads, while men were thrown overboard or jumped. The heavily laden French ships were wallowing and slow to manoeuvre, notably Eustace's ship carrying the heavy trebuchet. As a result, the English were able to defeat and capture most of the enemy fleet. It was a complete rout, with only 15 French ships surviving to get back to France. One estimate was that 4,000 French were killed, among them Eustace the Monk, although many of the other French knights were spared. For the French this was a devastating loss. After occupying nearly half the country and almost seeing the crown of England within his grasp, Prince Louis now had to sue for peace and leave. The English fleet, made rich from the Battle of Sandwich, donated part of the wealth to fund the Hospital of St Bartholomew in London, named after the saint's day on which the battle was fought.

BATTLE OF SLUYS

1340

The largest early medieval English naval battle was at Sluys, north of Zeebrugge, in 1340 in what is now the Netherlands. Edward III of England, who claimed the French throne, and Philip VI of France were involved in an ongoing war of attrition across the English Channel. French ships, aided by Genoese mercenaries, had successfully raided southern English ports and, in a blow to his pride, they had captured Edward III's largest ship, the Christopher, *when it was in Flanders. Determined to thwart Philip VI's ambitions to expand his territory and control the Channel, Edward III entered into an alliance with the Flemish, proclaimed himself king of France and set about assembling a fleet of ships to carry his army to that country. Merchant ships were brought in from ports around England to serve the king.*

Accounts vary but it is generally agreed that about 160 vessels set sail on 22 June from the River Orwell on the East Coast of England. Edward was on board his ship the *Cog Thomas* with 120 men. The intention was to attack the French fleet, which was known to be in the Flemish port of Sluys, on 23 June, but the tide was not right and there was a risk of grounding on the sandbanks. The next morning, with the tide working with them, the English ships headed into the river estuary to attack the French. The French had the advantage of a fleet of 204 ships, including many galleys which were easier to manoeuvre than large sailing ships, but they lost their advantage by deciding to chain their ships together in three great barrages across the river. Their tactic was to create a vast battle platform, as the traditional method of fighting at sea was to get near enough to attack at close quarters, supported by archers in the fore and aft castles of the ship. They would then grapple enemy ships and board with heavily armed soldiers. But by chaining their ships together in the narrow confines of the river the French became a static target for the English fleet.

The Battle of Sluys demonstrated France's lack of naval tactical acumen.

Their losses were enormous as the heavily armoured men fought hand-to-hand, but the English advantage was overwhelming. In the evening one French squadron from Dieppe fled the disaster, but was successfully pursued by England's Flemish allies. Jubilant, Edward III wrote to his son, Edward, Duke of Cornwall, on 28 June: 'Most dear son, we imagine that you will be glad to have good news of us'. He estimated 30,000 dead and reported the successful capture of 180 ships, including reclaiming his own ship, the *Christopher*. The Genoese mercenaries, led by their commander Pietro Barbavera, had wisely not lingered in the estuary with their French allies and had sailed out to sea, thus escaping the carnage. Barbavera's Mediterranean experience had given him a better sense of naval action than the French, who seemed to view the conflict through the lens of land battles.

The result was a crushing blow to French hopes of invading England, but they still had a very large land army and were able to reconstruct their fleet. After the battle Edward III landed and went on to an expensive but ineffective fight at Tournai. The Battle of Sluys did lead to a truce between Edward and Philip, and although French hit-and-run raids continued across the Channel Edward III could claim it as a mighty sea victory. At a time when gold coins were rare, he projected an image of national maritime glory by issuing a gold noble showing himself on board a ship (a cog prepared for war and displaying the arms of England and France).

BATTLE OF WINCHELSEA

1350

Edward III's great victory at Sluys did not ensure command of the sea. The French still had access to the Channel and the core of a professional naval force which was swift to act, unlike Edward who still relied on private ships which could take time to assemble. The French and their Castilian allies constantly threatened the coast and attacked shipping.

The French and English wars were halted briefly by a truce in 1341, but this came to an end in 1346 and Edward summoned one of the largest fleets ever known in England, not for battle but to carry his army overseas. Ships were commandeered from every port, large and small, across England, until a total of 655 vessels was gathered at Dartmouth. Devon sent 31, London 25 and Plymouth 26. The port supplying the largest single contingent was Fowey in Cornwall, with 47.

The original plan was to land in Gascony, southwest France, to meet the French army, but the management of such a large fleet combined with the weather made that unfeasible. So, on 12 July, Edward landed in the Normandy peninsula, captured Caen, destroyed the ships built to replace those lost at Sluys and won a great land battle at Crécy. This combination of land and seapower enabled him to target Calais, which he captured on 4 August 1347. A truce was subsequently agreed with France but this did not stop opportunistic raids across the Channel.

Ships were for carrying troops and equipment, not for fighting battles at sea. One type of vessel used for warlike purposes was the cog, a cargo ship used in northern Europe. It was flat bottomed, high sided and capable of carrying large loads, being strongly clinker built. Clinker building required the boards of the hull to be overlapped and fastened to one another, making a cumbersome but strong hull. An almost complete example was found in the mud of the river Weser near Bremen, Germany, in 1982.

In 1350 Edward and his son, known as the Black Prince, engaged in an unusual fight at sea. Attacking in harbour was the preferred tactic and was more effective, as in the battle of Sluys, so most sea battles were fought in sheltered, relatively shallow waters. Finding the enemy at sea was very difficult as intelligence often came too late and bringing ships alongside to fight one another in deep water was challenging, a fact highlighted by the Battle of Winchelsea.

Edward and his son were with their ships at Winchelsea, on the Sussex coast. They planned to intercept a Castilian fleet which had sailed to Flanders carrying a cargo of Spanish wool. Castile was now an ally of France and on its progress up the Channel it had taken several English ships as prizes. Edward learned that the Castilians had been sighted coming down the Channel with 47 ships under the command of Charles de la Cerda. These ships were much larger than the English ships and well prepared for action. Intercepting such a fleet at sea was an ambitious and difficult task as the ships of the day were single masted and lacking in manoeuvrability. Edward III was on board the *Cog Thomas* and ordered the master, Robert Passelow, 'To steer for that ship for I want to joust with her.' Steering for the target they collided heavily with it, severely damaging their own ship in the process and began to sink.

The contemporary chronicler Jean Froissart colourfully and rather romantically told the tale of this sea battle. He described the noise of the collision as sounding like thunder as the masts and castles of the two ships collided, sending the men in them into the sea. Water was pouring into the cog and the men manned the pumps and began to bail it out. Edward ordered his men to grapple the Spanish ship, saying 'I must have her!', but he was advised to 'Let her go, you'll get a better!' Indeed, another large enemy vessel came near, which they successfully grappled and boarded before the *Cog Thomas* totally sank. The Black Prince had a similar experience but he was rescued by the Earl of Derby's ship. Froissart describes the ships being grappled by the knights with iron hooks and chains and the Castilian archers in their castles raining arrows and hurling great iron bars.

The result of Winchelsea was not a major success; the English took several prizes and the Spanish lost 14 ships, but the Castilian fleet was still formidable. Later, civil war within Castile kept their ships from bothering the Channel for 20 years. Winchelsea was inevitably presented as a famous English victory but its fame was more to do with the personal involvement in it of Edward III and the Black Prince.

BATTLE OF LEPANTO

1571

---

*Lepanto was the last great battle between oar-driven
fleets, when a Christian coalition decisively beat
Ottoman Turks in a large galley fight off Western
Greece. In the sixteenth century, while the warship
was developing as a floating gun platform in the
Atlantic, the galley propelled by oars and with guns
mounted in the bows and stern remained popular in
the Mediterranean, with its fickle winds. The new
development in the middle of the sixteenth century
was the galleass, which would represent the next
phase of naval warfare. These were larger galleys,
but their oar power was augmented by three masts,
giving them greater power and manoeuvrability.*

Catholic Spain felt threatened by the Ottomans, who were gaining
territory across the Mediterranean. Fears of a possible invasion were
exacerbated by concerns that the converted Muslims (Moriscos)
who lived mainly in southern Spain might assist the Ottomans. The
Turkish fleets had command of much of the Eastern Mediterranean
and in 1570 they invaded Cyprus and besieged Famagusta, the
capital. Cyprus was then a possession of the Republic of Venice and
the Venetians had used Cyprus as a base from which to launch attacks
on Muslim pilgrim ships heading for Egypt and Mecca.

In the face of the perceived Ottoman threat, Pope Pius V organized a western alliance. His Holy League assembled more than 200 galleys and six galleasses and carried 28,000 soldiers, but facing them was the even larger Turkish fleet. The commander-in-chief of the Holy League was Don Juan of Austria, aged just 24 but already a competent and experienced leader on land and sea. He was well connected to the powerful Habsburgs as he was the illegitimate son of the late Charles V, Holy Roman Emperor, and half brother to Philip II of Spain. Don Juan had the challenge of knitting together a fleet consisting of Spain, the Papal States, the two great trading powers Genoa and Venice and the Knights of Malta. Venice, a great maritime city state, supplied the largest part of the fleet, with 107 galleys and six galleasses. This force began to assemble in the Strait of Messina between Sicily and Italy.

Both sides needed to know the strength of the other and there was an early miscalculation in naval intelligence. Ali Pasha, the Ottoman commander-in-chief, concentrated his fleet in the Gulf of Patras in Greece and sent a galley to spy on the assembled fleet at Messina. The galley, painted black and with black sails, gained access to Messina harbour and returned with news of the number of vessels involved. Unfortunately for the Turks, however, the information was incomplete, as Don Juan of Austria and the significant Spanish fleet had not yet arrived.

Don Juan's solution to his fleet of mixed nationalities was to organize five squadrons formed of vessels from most of the allies, but it was an uneasy alliance with constant petty disputes. He led the central group with 62 galleys, while on his left, with 53 galleys, was Agostino Barbarigo of Venice, and on his right was Andrea Doria of Genoa, with 50 galleys. Behind were seven fast galleys under Juan de Cardona of Spain, and then there was a reserve of 30 galleys under the Marquis of Santa Cruz. The Holy League's fleet sailed to Corfu and there they heard of the fall of Famagusta. They then moved to Cephalonia, close to the entrance of the Gulf of Petraeus, where the Turkish fleet was assembled.

The Battle of Lepanto took place on 7 October 1571 and involved up to 400 warships.

On 6 October both sides prepared to meet in battle, but each underestimated the strength of the other. The oared galleys were much in evidence, but there was a significant difference between the morale of the captive slaves in the Turkish fleet, for whom defeat could bring liberation, and the men manning the oars of the Holy League. Some of these men were hired while others, who were convicts, had been given the promise of pardon or remission of their sentence if victory was attained. There was also a difference in armaments, with the Turkish fleet having more bows and arrows than guns.

The Turks attacked while Don Juan's fleet was still arranging itself, the first assualt coming on the left where Barbarigo's squadron was almost overrun. There was close hand-to-hand fighting but eventually the Christian league began to overwhelm the attackers. In the centre there was again hand-to-hand fighting, but this time the conflict was even harder, with men boarding each other's ships. After two hours Ali Pasha was captured and killed by a triumphant Don Juan. On the right Andrea Doria's fleet appeared to be leaving the battle, pursued by El Loucke Ali, Viceroy of Algiers. With a gap opening up to the rear of the Holy League and Andrea Doria's squadron now out of range, El Loucke Ali then turned to attack the rear galleys of the centre, but Santa Cruz came to the rescue. El Loucke Ali escaped with what remained of his squadron. The fighting eventually came to an end after four hours, when Ali Pasha's whole crew had been killed. By the end of the battle the Holy League had lost 12 galleys, compared to 117 of the Ottomans, who had so gravely underestimated the power of their opponents. The Turkish fleet had been destroyed: 15 vessels had been sunk and 190 were taken as prizes. The death toll was high. Between 25,000 and 30,000 Turks are said to have been killed, while the Holy League estimated their losses at around 8,000. Ten thousand galley slaves were then released.

The Holy League had the benefit of better tactical use of artillery and better guns, including the firepower provided by the six new and heavy galleasses. This armament prevented the Ottomans from exploiting their skill in hand-to-hand fighting. Their underestimation of the size of the Holy League's fleet also led the Ottomans to be overconfident and force the battle. Historians have noted that the sultan's fleet was already exhausted as a result of its campaign that year, the galleys were undermanned due to earlier losses and many of the soldiers had already left for the winter.

The victory by the Holy League was widely celebrated and became the subject of many myths. Printing technology by now had become widespread and this ensured that news of this great victory for the Christian coalition was shared widely, often in simple woodcuts with the Ottomans frequently celebrated as heroic, worthy opponents. The battle was hailed as the end of the Muslim threat to Christianity, but it was indecisive in its outcome and the balance of power did not shift significantly in the Mediterranean.

The Ottomans soon recovered and by the spring of 1572 they had built 134 new vessels, complete with artillery, and had a navy of some 250 galleys and several smaller ships at their disposal. But they were stretched on many sides as they were also fighting in Persia and so were unable to continue their Mediterranean advance. Spanish resources were also stretched and were redirected to meet new challenges in the Netherlands. By 1580 a permanent truce was agreed with Spain. The Christian victory had, however, shown that the once invincible Ottoman navy could be defeated.

THE BATTLE OF GRAVELINES (SPANISH ARMADA)

1588

Tensions had been rising between Spain and England for some time. Although careful not to overly annoy her far more powerful rival, Elizabeth I supported Dutch rebels seeking independence from Spanish rule by providing infantry, cavalry and cash. In addition, London merchants were enraged by a Spanish embargo in 1585, which seized northern shipping in Spanish ports to use for an expedition. Although most of the affected shipping was Dutch, the English merchants responded to this act by calling for war.

The result was an expedition by Sir Francis Drake. In September 1585, he sailed from Plymouth with 29 ships and attacked and looted Spanish possessions in the West Indies, briefly touching down in Florida to destroy the Spanish fort of San Agustín. It was a shock to Spain and an affront to their reputation as a major power. Spain and England now considered themselves at war and, while Spain prepared an invasion, English ships stepped up their attacks. In 1587, Drake won notoriety for his attack on Cádiz, violating one of Spain's chief seaports. It delayed the Spanish preparations for the Armada and infuriated Philip II.

Elizabeth's fleet was composed of some new galleons and a number of large merchant ships, probably 40 vessels in all. However, with its vast empire, Spain had the largest merchant fleet in the world. Spanish and Portuguese merchants dominated oceanic trade, and with Spain's annexation of Portugal their vessels would bolster the Armada. But there was no bureaucratic structure to manage a navy and, as every decision went through King Philip (who relied on a small number of advisers), there was an administrative bottleneck.

The Spanish navy's main role was to seize and hold a base in England so the soldiers could land. Philip's battle commander was the Marquis of Santa Cruz, whose invasion of Terceira in the Azores in 1582 was a classic example of his careful planning. Santa Cruz wanted to repeat this successful invasion in England and estimated that it would take a landing force of 55,000 troops. This would require an enormous number of ships, nearly 80,000 tons, plus galleys and more than 200 landing craft. The plan was to land on the Kent coast and advance on London. But Philip's nephew, the Duke of Parma, had an alternative vision of a speedy invasion force from Flanders, which required large numbers of troops on barges landing in England. Philip decided to merge both plans. A smaller armada would sail from Lisbon to meet the Flemish force and they would then combine to attack across the Channel, a plan that satisfied neither commander. Both could see the challenge of trying to coordinate the meeting of two large forces thousands of miles apart.

The great commander Santa Cruz died in January 1588 and was succeeded by the Duke of Medina Sidonia as the overall commander. A senior nobleman and a talented administrator, Sidonia brought his skills to bear on finalizing the provisioning and equipping of the Armada. It finally left Lisbon on 18 May and comprised around 127 ships carrying around 30,000 men, the majority of whom were soldiers.

Initially scattered by poor weather off Corunna (now A Coruña), the Armada regrouped and headed up the English Channel. Sidonia had little faith in the whole enterprise and indeed had urged to Philip to cancel it, but Philip believed he had God on his side. He wrote to the Duke in April 1588, 'if you do not encounter the enemy until you reach Margate, you should find there the Admiral of England with his fleet alone – or even if he should have united with Drake's fleet, yours will still be superior to both in quality, and also in the cause you are defending which is God's.'

The large Spanish ships were floating fortresses filled with troops and designed for close-quarter boarding engagements, not gun battles at sea. The battle order was based on galley warfare. Strong warships, including the flagship, were at the centre; the fighting ships were at the rear of the group; and between them were the supply ships and the heavy transport. The hub was the flagship, and each part of the Armada was required to keep its appointed place in relation to that vessel. There was also a small group of around 20 ships that were permitted to move from their formation to deal with problems.

The English knew that invasion troops were waiting on the Flemish Coast and that there was an armada on its way, but little more detail was available. The English ships were not as big as the Spanish warships and the English had developed sea fighting in a different way, with smaller, lighter vessels as gun platforms. They also had a big advantage in the on-board command structure. Drake had initiated the idea of the whole crew acting together as a company under a single sea captain, whereas the Spanish system was overloaded with aristocratic officers and the chain of command was not clear.

In overall command of the English fleet was Lord Howard of Effingham. While Sir Francis Drake was the premier and most experienced fighting commander, he was actually second-in-command. Howard's appointment owed much to his close personal relationship with the queen, but he was also an able and effective diplomat. Although he was Lord Admiral of England, he had limited sea experience, so

Howard appointed some of the great sea captains to his war council. In addition to Drake there were John Hawkins, Martin Frobisher and Thomas Fenner. Devon and Cornwall were the frontline against the impending attack, and Sir Richard Grenville and Sir Walter Raleigh were appointed to plan the defence of the West Country. Arms and equipment were prepared, armed men were placed along the southern coast and a series of fire beacons was made ready to announce the enemy fleet's arrival. To contemporaries such as Sir Richard Carew the Spanish fleet seemed a mighty 'heaven-threatening Armado'.

Howard's council urged him to take the initiative and tackle the Spanish fleet on the Spanish coast to prevent their plans. Constrained by a lack of finance, Elizabeth refused and would only allow the fleet to patrol the seas. Howard managed to spread his ships between the Scillies and Ushant in an attempt to get an early glimpse of the Spanish fleet, but bad weather in June and July detained the English in Plymouth harbour. Lord Howard, while battling to get funding to feed his men and to stop crews from deserting, kept up a regular correspondence with the queen and her advisers. His frustration at her caution – and apparent parsimony in the face of such a serious national threat – broke through on 23 June when he wrote, 'For the love of Jesus Christ, Madam, awake thoroughly, and see the villainous treasons roundabout you.' Rumours abounded about the Spanish plans while the English fleet lay in Plymouth, ready and waiting.

The great Spanish Armada sighted the Lizard at 4 pm in the afternoon on 19 July 1588, when the royal standard was raised on the flagship the *San Martin*, together with a sacred banner depicting the Virgin Mary and St Mary Magdalene. The next day the Spanish came across a boat out of Falmouth with four fishermen on board, whom they captured and interrogated. The fishermen insisted, either deliberately or merely repeating a rumour, that the English fleet had already set sail from Plymouth.

By the time of the Armada ships were more manoeuvrable, with more masts and sails. Oared galleys were still used, but from 1545

The Battle of Gravelines, on 7 August, led to the final defeat of the Armada. Gravelines is the French coastal town between Calais and Dunkirk off which the battle took place.

onwards the tactical use of guns was changing and it was now possible to sink another ship using long-range firing. The English, with their considerable privateering experience, favoured fast, mobile and well-armed ships, but Drake was aware that the heavily-gunned Spanish ships could inflict serious damage on the lighter English ships. At the same time, the English guns were unlikely to inflict major damage at long range. It was not obvious to Howard or Drake how they might break the Spanish formation or impede its progress up the Channel. Hearing the news of the approach of the Spanish fleet, they got their ships to sea on 20 July. This took all night, as the wind and currents were unfavourable, so they had to warp, or haul, the ships out.

Rather than one big sea battle, much of the initial action in the Channel was a series of skirmishes as the English sought to come up with a plan to stop the Armada from landing or from heading further up the English Channel. The Spanish were under strict instructions to maintain their relative positions in the formation, while the English had quite different orders from Howard: 'Lastly, forasmuch as there may fall out many accidents that, may move you to take any other course than by these our instructions you are directed, we therefore think it most expedient to refer you therein to your own judgement and discretion, to do that thing you may think may best attend to the advancement of our service.'

The fleets met in the early afternoon of 20 July, and the English attacked each wing of the Spanish formation. These wings had their best fighting ships and the only casualties were accidental. The *San Salvador* was damaged by a gunpowder explosion and was abandoned, while the *Nuestra Señora del Rosario* was damaged in a collision, losing her bowsprit. Drake was able to capture the *Rosario* the next morning, including her commander, Don Pedro de Valdes, the ship's company and a pay chest with 50,000 ducats. Such a valuable prize for Drake did not endear him to his fellow commanders, who suspected him of acting more like a privateer. Examination of the *Rosario*, however, also brought detailed information about the Spanish artillery with its heavy and cumbersome two-wheeled carriages that were arduous to manage. English guns, by contrast, were mounted on four-wheeled carriages and could be continuously fired, while the English gunners were well-trained.

There was a week of fighting down the Channel, but the Spanish fleet remained largely intact and continued its stately progress. Sidonia was tempted to shelter near the Solent, but attacks by Drake at Portland Bill on 23 July and the Isle of Wight on 25 July forced him to abandon this idea and continue up the Channel. Communications were challenging for the Armada. Sidonia had sent several messages to Parma's headquarters in Bruges, but had as yet received no reply. Not wishing to be swept on into the North Sea, the Spanish fleet anchored off Calais, uncertain where to rendezvous with Parma.

The situation was now something of a stalemate: the English were unable to break the Spanish formation and the Spaniards had lost just three of their ships. The guns of the English fleet – now reinforced to about 140 vessels – were not causing significant damage to the heavily built Spanish vessels, while the Spanish were finding the English ships too swift to have the chance to grapple with them. The English needed to come up with a new plan. With the two fleets anchored less than 2 miles (3.2 km) from each other, Howard convened a council of war. The conclusion was to break the impasse with fire ships. Eight smaller ships were selected and, just after midnight, the Spaniards saw the vessels bearing down on them with the tide. This tactic was effective, causing considerable chaos, although the Spanish were able to deflect two of the fire ships. By then, many ships in the Spanish fleet had to cut their anchors and move out to sea, scattering the Armada at last. At daybreak, just off Gravelines, Drake led a close-range artillery assault on the remaining ships, which comprised Medina Sidonia's flagship, and five big ships. Here, the English gunnery prevailed: the English were able to fire one or one-and-a-half rounds an hour per gun; the Spanish could only manage the equivalent in one day.

That night the English drove the Spaniards further into shallow water but, just when the English attack might have driven the Spanish fleet ashore, the wind suddenly veered, enabling the Spanish to escape into the North Sea. Howard wrote to Elizabeth's chief adviser, Robert Cecil, on 27 August, 'Myself, with the rest of her Majesty's fleet, do here wait for a wind that may give us liberty to go look upon these bravoes, and then I doubt not but to make them wish themselves at home in an ill harbour.' The Armada regrouped and headed up the north coast of England pursued by Howard's ships. Both sides were now short of ammunition. In Howard's words, 'we put on a brag countenance and gave them chase.' Once the Spanish had reached the Scottish coast, the English returned to the Thames Estuary, having neither the armament nor the powder to engage the enemy.

Elizabeth took the lead in celebrating the great victory, graciously accepting the heartfelt thanks of her subjects, but now washed her hands of anything further to do with her victorious fleet and its mariners. Howard was not so ready to ignore his responsibilities and his help was badly needed, as typhoid fever swept through the ships. Urging the queen to keep the fleet intact until they knew the ultimate fate of the Spanish fleet, Howard personally paid for fresh victuals for the starving mariners and found them accommodation on shore at Dover, even selling some of his own belongings to buy clothing for the men. Going further, he requisitioned part of Drake's plunder from the *Rosario*, saying: 'and had it not been mere necessity, I would not have touched [it]; but if I had not some to have bestowed upon some poor and miserable men, I should have wished myself out of the world.' As Howard prepared to return to court, he wisely reflected that 'if men should not be cared for better than to let them starve and die miserably, we should very hardly get men to serve.'

The long haul around the northern isles finally put paid to Spanish invasion plans. They faced a long voyage with damaged ships, many casualties, and were short of food and water and exhausted and demoralized. To his credit, Medina Sidonia returned with 67 ships, among them some of the best warships, but they were badly damaged, and one third of the total manpower of the Armada failed to return.

The English could claim a great victory against the dominant Spanish power, and, as one historian put it, 'that formidable combination, sailing ship and the broadside gun, would dominate England's global destiny for the next 250 years.' Spain went into mourning, and her enemies were encouraged by the shattering of Spain's previous invincibility. The English continued with fresh attacks and an increased sense of confidence in their destiny at sea.

BATTLE OF CÁDIZ

1596

*Elizabeth I had seen her country successfully defend
itself from a Spanish invasion force in 1588, but the
threat remained and in 1596 she sent an expedition
to attack one of the key ports in mainland Spain.
She was then aged 63 and had been on the throne
for 38 years. Before Lord Howard's expedition set
out, Elizabeth composed a special prayer:*

*Thou that by this foresight does truly discern how no malice
of revenge nor questions of injury, nor desire of bloodshed nor
greediness of lucre, hath bred the resolution of our now set out
army, but heed full care and a weary watch.*

Unlike Drake's West Indies expeditions, which were financed largely
by private money on a joint-stock basis, this expedition was entirely
paid for by Elizabeth. There was growing anxiety about Spanish naval
preparations, so while other expeditions had targeted Spanish silver
fleets this was a deliberate pre-emptive strike against the Spanish
navy. The great naval commanders Drake and Hawkins were dead,
but Lord Admiral Howard was still in command. He was in personal
charge of this expedition and his task was clear:

*By burning of ships of war in his havens before they should
come forth to the seas, and therewith also destroying his*

magazines of victuals and his munitions for the arming of his Navy, to provide that neither the rebels in Ireland should be aided and strengthened, nor yet the king be able, of long time, to have any great Navy in readiness to offend us.

Howard sailed from Plymouth on 1 June with 100 sailing vessels, including the necessary transport ships carrying troops. In the fleet were 17 of the queen's ships and also a Dutch squadron under Johan van Duivenvoorde, operating with the English for the first time. Maintaining strict secrecy, Howard did not give out his sealed orders until they were off Cape Ortegal, Spain. Such a large fleet was hard to hide, so they captured any passing vessels which might have raised the alarm. For the Spanish, the first intimation of the attacking fleet was when they watched it rounding Cape St Vincent.

Cádiz is an island with open water on three sides and the fleet anchored off Cádiz on 20 June and waited for the high tide. They attacked at dawn the following morning. Howard and his captains managed a difficult combined operation with professionalism while the English navy continued to learn lessons from war and became more efficient in many ways. All of the Spanish warships were either taken or destroyed and English troops, led by the flamboyant and impetuous favourite of the queen, Lord Essex, captured the city. It was a great success, marred only slightly by missing the chance to capture an outward-bound flota (fleet) with its valuable cargo, as the ships were set on fire by their own crews.

The discipline of the English troops was remarkable for the time and the inhabitants of the fallen city were treated humanely. The Duke of Medina Sidonia arrived in the area after the city had fallen and Howard, in an elegant Latin letter about an exchange of prisoners, could not resist reminding the duke of a previous encounter. 'As I was entrusted with the command by my Lady the Queen's Majesty in the year 1588, I suppose I may not be unknown to you...'

Essex was keen to hold Cádiz permanently and was supported

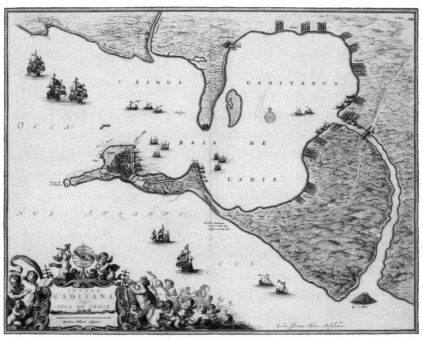

Map of the Bay of Cádiz. Although the bay was well-protected, Cádiz's defenders were unprepared for the Anglo-Dutch attack and had to burn their own ships to stop them from being taken.

by Duivenvoorde, both men thinking that trade from the West and East Indies could be severely disrupted, but Howard overruled them. He did not have orders for such an action and there was also an awareness of the difficulty of maintaining a hold on Cádiz from a distance. The expedition returned after destroying fortifications and public buildings, leaving the burnt remains of 13 warships, 11 West Indies ships and many smaller vessels.

They arrived in England with two new Spanish warships, 12,000 pieces of ordnance and looted goods which were estimated by the Spanish as being worth in excess of 20 million ducats. Among the coin, plate, quantities of pearls, silks, sugar and other items were books. Howard's chaplain, Edward Doughty, took 17 theological works from the Jesuit College and later presented them to Hereford Cathedral, where they remain. Essex was bolder. He took the complete library of the Bishop of Faro and gave it to a new library in Oxford being established by Thomas Bodley, now the Bodleian library. Elizabeth recovered just £12,000 in coin and plate.

The loss of Cádiz was a major financial catastrophe for Spain. The silver fleets were disrupted and the capture of such a notable location on the mainland had serious political implications. Philip ordered his fleet to attack England immediately, and in just three months Martín de Padilla led a fleet of 160 warships into the English Channel. The attack could have been highly successful as the English ships were refitting at Chatham and there was little in the way of defence in the West Country, but again the weather disrupted the Spanish plans. Southwesterly gales caught the armada off the Galician coast, where they lost 30 of their large warships; the rest of the fleet had to run for shelter in port. It was the end of Spanish ambitions to conquer England; within two years Philip II of Spain was dead, followed five years later by his sister-in-law, Elizabeth I.

FIRST ANGLO-DUTCH WAR

1652–1654

The two great trading nations of the 1660s were the English and the Dutch and they fought three naval wars in the second half of the seventeenth century, mainly in the North Sea and the English Channel. England had supported the Dutch during their fight for independence from Spain, and by the mid-seventeenth century they were a great trading nation. The Dutch commercial network stretched across the Atlantic to North and South America and east as far as Japan. Their navy rivalled the English Navy in both the English Channel and the North Sea, and had pushed the English out of the Baltic as the main carriers of timber. The Dutch East India company, the VOC, halted the English East India Company's eastward expansion, leaving it to fall back on India. Under severe pressure from the increasingly powerful merchant class, the English Commonwealth passed the first Navigation Act in 1651, with the aim of limiting British trade to British ships, while the Dutch, however, advocated open trade.

It was during this time that the sailing battle fleet gained importance. Previously, fleets were put together at a time of crisis and then disbanded, but now privateering was a threat and it had become very effective. Private, well-armed ships that attacked the enemy's merchant ships caused merchant ships to organize into convoys and they needed protection by state vessels. The state fleets contained large, heavily armed ships but also required the addition of armed merchantmen.

There were many battles and quite a few were indecisive in their outcome, but over the period valuable lessons were learnt about tactics, discipline and administration in sailing navies. The Battle of Goodwin Sands in 1652 is not particularly well reported and it began before the English or the Dutch had declared war. It was mainly the result of actions by the men on the scene, rather than major political decisions, and was quite unplanned.

1652 Battle of Goodwin Sands

It was a time of great tension between the two mercantile nations. Parliament laid claim to the English Channel as English territorial waters and foreign ships, when confronted by English men-of-war, were expected to lower their national flags as a sign of deference. The English, in search of contraband, also required neutral ships to comply with a stop and search policy. A few days before the incident at Goodwin Sands, a Dutch convoy had been attacked by a small English squadron when the men-of-war escort refused to lower its flag.

Lieutenant Admiral Maarten Tromp arrived off Goodwin Sands with his fleet of 40 sail and protested to a small squadron of English ships under the command of Major Nehemiah Bourne that they were merely sheltering from bad weather. Naval fleets frequently met potential enemies while in the open sea and, in a time of high tension between nations, the combatants on board had no speedy way of establishing whether the situation on land had changed or even if there had been an official declaration of war. It is not clear who fired first, but it was the opening salvo of the First Anglo-Dutch War.

Bourne alerted Robert Blake, the General-at-Sea, who was at that time at Rye with his squadron of 14 ships. Tromp, meanwhile, anchored just off Dover and ignored all of the warning shots from Dover Castle on the clifftop, which attempted to remind him to strike his flag. He then remained overnight. In the morning the Dutch fleet saw Blake's squadron heading towards them from Rye and Tromp wisely left and sailed towards Calais, taking a course between Blake's squadron in the south and Bourne and his ships in the north. What followed next has never been explained. Tromp, who could have escaped, decided to attack Blake's squadron and battle commenced, with Bourne leading his squadron and effectively trapping the Dutch. It was an indecisive and scrappy battle that lasted into the night. Tromp escaped but he lost two vessels, while the English lost none.

1652 Battle of Kentish Knock

With the two nations now officially at war, the English sought to destroy the Dutch Navy and halt their successful commercial activities. However, the Dutch were determined to protect their sailing convoys and a fleet of 60 ships was sent to ensure safe passage for Dutch merchant ships in the English Channel, under the command of Vice Admiral Witte Corneliszoon de With. Admiral Blake of the English Navy had a fleet of 68 ships and the two fleets met off Kentish Knock in September 1652, on the approach to the Thames Estuary. The Dutch opened fire and several of Blake's ships ran aground on the sandbanks, but the English put up a strong resistance and caused damage and casualties to the Dutch. The Dutch then attacked the English fleet to the south, but Vice Admiral Sir William Penn counter-attacked. After three hours of heavy intensive combat, the Dutch withdrew as night fell. They had again lost two ships while the English claimed victory, since they had not lost a single ship.

The Dutch States General formed another fleet of 73 ships and again put Admiral Tromp in command, with orders to 'do all possible harm to the English' while protecting large convoys. These convoys

Robert Blake, General-at-Sea, oversaw England's navy in the First Anglo-Dutch War. A great commander, some consider him the country's greatest-ever admiral, with one historian claiming that 'his successes have never been excelled, not even by Nelson.'

were sailing along the Channel carrying goods to and from Dutch possessions in America, the West Indies and the Far East.

1652 Battle of Dungeness

Blake was anchored in the Downs with a fleet of 37 ships when he saw Tromp's fleet in November. It is possible that Blake was unaware of the size of the forces against him but he set sail to attack. The winds, however, were too strong to enable the two fleets to engage and they were both blown towards the southwest. As the fleets were near Dungeness the next morning Blake was trapped and was forced to fight. This time the Dutch claimed victory, with three English ships sunk and just one Dutch ship lost. Tromp was able to safely escort a convoy of 400 merchant ships through the Channel and into the Atlantic.

This battle generated new activity from the English Council of State, who sent reinforcements to Blake from the army in the form of General Richard Deane and General George Monck, who became joint commanders. The fleet was a mixture of government vessels and armed merchant vessels and the latter were suspected of being more interested in preserving their vessels than pressing forward in battle. Six English captains were dismissed for failing to support Blake. Additionally, there were concerns about the loyalties of men who had so recently been at war with one another in England. A new code of discipline was published and naval officers were put in command of armed merchantmen. Seamen were encouraged by new pay scales, plans to care for the sick and wounded and prize regulations changed to ensure that seamen would benefit from capturing a Dutch man-of-war as much as a merchant vessel. Additionally, the Council concentrated all of the naval shipping into the Channel, abandoning those destined to protect trade in the Mediterranean.

1653 Battle of Portland Bill

Sometimes known as the Three Day Battle, this was a series of engagements rather than one set piece confrontation. Admiral Tromp was

The Battle of Kentish Knock was the first official clash of rival navies in the First Anglo-Dutch War, on 28 September 1652.

escorting a convoy of 150 merchant ships east through the Channel. He had 81 ships to protect them and on 18 February they saw an English force of the same size heading their way. Due to the wind conditions, Tromp had an opportunity to get away but chose instead to turn and fight the leading English ships. The three English squadrons became separated. Blake's squadron, which had been surging ahead, was surrounded and almost overwhelmed by the Dutch, but his large heavy ships held their own until the other two squadrons joined him. The fighting was a melee, with ships getting in close and boarding and counter-boarding each other. Eventually, the English pushed back against the Dutch and threatened the convoy, which forced Tromp to break away. Over the next three days the two fleets manoeuvred against one another up and down the Channel. Tromp was able to use his knowledge to take the convoy through shallow waters, knowing the larger English ships could not follow. He and most of the convoy eventually escaped but they had lost between 30 and 60 merchant ships, while the English had captured four warships and five others had sunk. The English lost just one ship and three were damaged.

Most of these meetings have been described as extremely chaotic. The perceived wisdom by both fleets was to organize into squadrons: a leading squadron or van, a central squadron which had the commander within it and a rear admiral in the third squadron. Each ship was ordered to maintain its place relative to the leader of the squadron, which was no easy feat in the midst of a battle between sailing ships. Communication between the commander and his ships was also difficult. Keeping control of a mixture of ships during the battle, whose crews had different skills and experience, together with smoke from the cannons and intermingling with the enemy, was almost impossible. It was difficult to see the signals from the leader of the squadron, let alone the commander-in-chief. In March 1653 new instructions were issued to the English Navy, which defined the signals and also laid out instructions for the line of battle. This presented the enemy with a powerful broadside, thus favouring the power of English gunnery. The instructions emphasized the need for the fleet to 'manoeuvre and fight in a supportive manner'. These became the basis for naval tactics and discipline for the next century and a half.

1653 Battle of the Gabbard or North Foreland

Tromp and the Dutch fleet were at sea again in May and the English set out in pursuit. They finally saw each other in the Thames estuary near Harwich. As they counted each other's fleets they were evenly matched with 98 Dutch ships to 100 English ships. Led by Deane and Monck, the English put their new instructions to good use, forming a crescent shape, and the battle began mid-morning. The initial broadside from the Dutch killed Deane as he stood on HMS *Resolution*. It was only General Monck's second naval battle and now he was suddenly in overall command. The English fleet maintained the windward position for much of the engagement, forcing the Dutch to sail parallel and use their guns. The preferred tactic of the Dutch was to get close and board ships, while the English relied on their gunnery skills. The gun battle went into the second day and, low on ammunition and with a badly damaged fleet, Tromp disengaged. It was a decisive defeat compared to previous skirmishes, with the English losing no ships and sustaining 400 casualties, whereas Tromp's fleet had lost 20 ships in total, of which 11 were captured. It was also a victory for the new English battle order, as one English participant commented: 'Our fleet did work better order than heretofore, and seconded one another.'

1653 Battle of Scheveningen

Despite sustaining high losses the Dutch managed to rebuild their fleet in rapid time and in July 1653 Tromp and a fleet of 125 ships met Monck off Texel in the Battle of Scheveningen. Again the English

The Battle of Scheveningen. This engagement was initiated by the Dutch as an attempt to break England's blockade of their ports. Although technically a win for the English, the losses incurred on both sides led to peace negotiations and an end to the First Anglo-Dutch War – and, as the Dutch had hoped, a lifting of the trade blockade against them.

were successful, although the fleets this time were less ordered, with each side passing through each other on more than one occasion. The great leader, Admiral Tromp, was killed during the battle and the Dutch lost approximately 30 ships, while the English lost just two. But the English paid a heavier price with around 1,000 men killed or wounded, more than in previous battles. The two final battles of the First Dutch War showed the success of the developing ideas of line of battle combined with effective gunnery. In the Scheveningen battle the English had used a combination of line of battle followed by melee tactics, which led to the higher casualties. However, in the autumn severe weather caused major damage to the remaining Dutch fleet and the States General had to open negotiations. By the following year the First Anglo-Dutch War was over.

BATTLE OF SANTA CRUZ DE TENERIFE

1657

*Following the privateering activities of the
Elizabethans, the seventeenth century saw an
embryo English navy develop during and after
the Civil War, as it began to operate from the
Mediterranean to North America and the West
Indies. It also expanded its types of operation, and
in Tenerife in 1657 this included attacking shore
fortifications and ships at anchor. In March 1656
Robert Blake, the General-at-Sea, was cruising
off the coast of Spain. The target was as ever the
Spanish flota as it brought its valuable cargo of
bullion back to Spain. The successful capture of
this target would bring much-needed relief to the
financially stretched English Republic and enable it
to pay its armies and fleets.*

Blake had found the Spanish elusive, although Rear Admiral Richard
Stayner did manage to capture two large galleons in September. In
an unusual move for the time, Blake decided to keep his ships at sea
through the winter so they could be in place for early news of the
approach of the next flota. In effect, this became a blockade and it
forced the Spanish to change tactics by putting their 11 ships into the

Canary Islands. Here they could wait until the English abandoned the blockade or the Dutch gave them escort assistance.

Hearing that the Spanish were at Santa Cruz on the island of Tenerife, in April 1657 Blake sailed with the whole of his fleet, gambling that the Spanish fleet in Cádiz would not be able to escape from the bay in time. His captains were unhappy, however, having been denied opportunities for prizes by their cautious commander, and there had been robust and forceful disagreements between them. Blake called a meeting as they arrived off Tenerife. Rear Admiral Richard Stayner's report of the action noted that 'The general called the council to know what we should do, the commanders having displeased him so much the Saturday before said never a word until he earnestly desired them.'

A plan emerged and Blake ordered four ships from each squadron to come together. These 12 ships, led by Rear Admiral Stayner, would enter the bay and attack the moored Spanish ships, while Blake and the rest of the fleet remained just outside with covering fire and planned to 'batter up castles'. The Bay of Santa Cruz was heavily defended with forts and gun batteries to protect the valuable fleet and the winds were often unpredictable in the bay so that ships entering it might not be able to exit safely.

Stayner's orders to the captains told them when they were to follow him and in a later account he wrote that he told them that 'wheresoever I saw the greatest danger I would go, and that they fired not a gun until they were at an anchor'. In his flagship, *Speaker*, Stayner led the ships in the early morning of 20 April and was fortunate to discover that some of the Spanish ships were moored between the incoming vessels and the shore, so that the shore batteries risked attacking their own vessels. With great discipline the English fleet attacked the inner line of small vessels and then turned its attention to the seven large galleons.

At around midday Blake and the second set of English vessels entered the bay and by 1 pm all Spanish vessels had been captured or destroyed and the forts had been neutralized by accurate fire from the attackers. Blake now had his victory but he still had to get back to sea. Five of the English ships were trying to tow captured vessels. These had the potential to provide considerable prize money but the tow was challenged by the winds and some Spanish batteries were still firing. Blake ordered that the prizes be set on fire and abandoned and, eventually and reluctantly, his captains complied. That afternoon the English fleet slowly managed to clear the bay. Stayner's ship, *Speaker*, was the worst damaged. A tow from another ship failed, so they had to remain there at great risk from the onshore batteries. The wind changed in the very late afternoon and setting what little scraps of sail they had they cut their anchor and headed out, passing under 'the great Castle ... and we were forced to keep our guns going still and the enemy plying hard at us', but 'either by our shot or some accident among themselves, there was a great quantity of powder blown up; after that they never fired one gun more at us'. They reached safety as dusk fell, at which point all of their damaged masts fell overboard.

It was a highly praised victory. Blake lost 60 men and around 140 were wounded, but no ships were lost despite the heaviness of the attack. On the other hand, all of the Spanish ships had been destroyed, despite being aided by a heavily defended harbour and adverse winds.

While the English Republican Parliament was loud in its praise of 'God's marvellous goodness', the great financial prize eluded them as the Spanish had landed the bullion before the attack and hidden it inland. But the Spanish did not benefit from the bullion either, as it remained on Tenerife. Short of pay, the Spanish army deserted during its offensive against Portugal and Spain reluctantly recognized Portugal's independence in 1667. Similarly, lack of money with which to pay the Spanish army in Flanders also weakened Spain. Spain was no longer a great power and its golden age was coming to an end.

SECOND ANGLO-DUTCH WAR

1665-1667

Seventeenth-century naval fleets were still a mixed bag of ship types, and captains' abilities were even more mixed. Several fleets still had merchant captains at the helm. In the midst of battle it was not unknown for these merchant marines to go after rich crippled prizes rather than stay in formation. Professional navies were, however, beginning to emerge. Naval administration was growing but was subject to severe delay and corrupt practices, while the science of naval architecture was also developing and revised articles had been issued. The monarchy had been restored under Charles II, who was attempting to bring stability to England. He was reluctant to go to war with the Dutch but his merchant class were alarmed by continuing Dutch commercial success. Instead, Charles authorized smaller expeditions. One, led by his brother, the Duke of York, captured the Dutch city of New Amsterdam in North America in August 1664 and renamed it New York. Partly for economic reasons but also due to factional struggles in the court of King Charles, the Second Anglo-Dutch War was declared in March 1665.

View of New Amsterdam in 1664. Captured by the English that same year, the North American city was renamed New York and became one of the bases for further English expansion into the American interior.

1665 Battle of Lowestoft

The Dutch were at sea in May and their commander, Admiral Jacob van Wassenaer Obdam, had orders to defeat the English. The two fleets were evenly matched with around 100 ships each but they were differently organized. For political reasons, the Dutch had no less than 21 divisions, each with its own flag officer, arranged into seven squadrons. The English had three squadrons under James, Duke of York, in overall command and leading the centre squadron. Prince Rupert was leading the van and the Earl of Sandwich led the rear. The English went into battle in line, but it did not remain that way. The fight became confused as the fleets engaged, with each side passing through the line on several occasions, more by accident than design. At one stage of the battle the Duke of York in his flagship *Royal Charles* was battling directly with Admiral Obdam in the *Eendracht*. The Duke of York nearly lost his life in his first sea engagement, when chain-shot swept across his quarterdeck, killing several of his courtiers. Admiral Obdam was killed by a cannon shot and shortly afterwards the magazine in his ship exploded, killing many of its crew. Leaderless, the Dutch retreated in confusion. That night, rather than press after the retreating Dutch, the *Royal Charles* pulled back, possibly to ensure belatedly the safety of the Duke of York, who was heir to the throne. At the end of the confrontation 4,000 Dutch had been killed or wounded and another 2,000 were prisoners. The Dutch had also lost 32 ships while the English had lost just one ship and suffered nearly 900 casualties. The first engagement of the war saw the English gain control of the sea and the clear victory gave their navy a new-found confidence.

In June 1666, General Monck and Prince Rupert were the joint commanders as they sailed to intercept enemy fleets. Prince Rupert, the nephew of Charles II, was a highly experienced captain. A decision was made to divide the fleet and Prince Rupert led his squadron to the west to intercept the French, who were now allied with the Dutch. With a group of 54 ships, Monck, now the Duke of Albemarle, headed towards Admiral de Ruyter's fleet of 84 ships in the English Channel between Ostend and Harwich. Despite the superior size of the Dutch fleet, Albemarle went on the offensive in a long and bloody battle of attrition that became known as the Four Days' Battle. Outnumbered and facing a better tactician in Admiral de Ruyter, the battle ended in defeat for the smaller English fleet, which lost ten ships of the line, while six fireships and ten ships were also captured. The Dutch lost four ships of the line and five fireships. There were recriminations in England, but the conflict continued and both sides began to re-equip quickly.

1666 St James's Day Fight

By July both sides had new ships, proving the resilience of their respective shipbuilders. In England additional instructions, including signals, were issued by Prince Rupert, plus revised fighting instructions were authorized by the Duke of York. These insisted that the fleet 'keep the enemy to leeward … And to take special care that they keep their line, and upon pain of death that they fire not over any of our own ships'. While having the wind was a known tactic, it was now seen as essential in gaining the advantage in battle.

At four o'clock in the afternoon of 24 July the two fleets saw each other. The English in total had 81 ships of war of which 23 were new and the Dutch had 88 ships including eight new ships of war. The next day, 25 July, St James Day, the fleets were organized. The leading squadron or van (Red), was commanded by Sir Thomas Allin. Prince Rupert and Albemarle were on the Royal Charles *in the centre (White) and at the rear (Blue) the squadron was commanded by Sir Jeremy Smith. The Dutch van was led by Admiral Johan Evertsen, in the centre was de Ruyter and Cornelis Tromp, son of the late Admiral Maarten Tromp, had the rear.*

Battle commenced around 10 am and Vice Admiral Sir Thomas Teddiman's ship, *Royal Catherine*, was the first English ship to be fired on by the Dutch. The two leading squadrons engaged each other very closely. An early death was that of Evertsen, the Dutch commander, and it caused his flagship to run into five others. The two centre squadrons engaged at 11 am, firing broadsides as they edged closer until they were within musket shot. It was carnage, with shot and fireships used by both sides. 'The noise of guns was heard in London all day while in Bruges the houses and beds were reported to have been shaken by the cannon's thunder,' noted one observer.

It may seem odd to modern eyes, but it was not a constant fight and it was not always clear which ships were where. Ships could withdraw from the front line to make repairs and then return. The *Royal Charles* and the *Henry* had to withdraw for repairs. Surgeon-General James Pearse witnessed the battle:

> *About three our Admiral came out of the line and lay about an hour to repair his damages and the* Sovereign *fell into his place. Soon after de Ruyter's fire ship was sunk and his main topmast being shot down bore into his fleet before the wind. Between three and four the* Henry *came out of the line, both his topmasts disabled.*
>
> *About this time their whole fleet bore away before the wind except those that broke in between the Red and Blue squadron. About four we saw a ship burn near our general's which we judge to be a fire ship of ours. About half an hour after we saw a ship blow up near the* Royal Oak *which we judged to be one of theirs.*

The *Royal Charles*, repaired, moved back towards de Ruyter's ship and thick smoke enveloped the vessels. The English rear squadron, the Blue, had engaged at midday and Tromp's squadron initially had a slight advantage. On his own initiative, he had led the Dutch rear division through a gap and forced a melee. About 4 pm de Ruyter, with seven remaining ships, followed his retreating van southeast, pursued by the English.

The chase continued the next day, but with no general action the Dutch van and centre reached Flushing. Tromp was still, however, only 30 miles (48 km) away, but he eventually managed to elude the English and join de Ruyter on 27 July.

The casualties sustained by the Dutch were particularly high, numbering around 4,000 killed and 3,000 wounded, while the English reported around 300–500 men lost. Twenty Dutch ships were lost but the English lost just one, the *Resolution*. Additionally, the Dutch lost many naval leaders, five flag officers and several captains.

In the days following the battle de Ruyter accused Tromp of dereliction of duty, and Tromp retaliated with accusations that his squadron had been deserted. As a result, Tromp was dismissed. In England, Sir Jeremy Smith, commanding the rear, was blamed for allowing Tromp to escape, but he was defended by Albemarle and Charles II exonerated him. The national rejoicing over such a comprehensive victory was not destined to last for long.

1667 Dutch raid on the Medway

In May 1667, shortage of money caused Charles II to order the English fleet to be laid up, with the larger ships towed up the Medway near the naval dockyard at Chatham. As peace plans were being prepared the Dutch politician Johan de Witt had other plans in mind and was plotting a raid.

On 7 June the Dutch fleet anchored off the mouth of the Thames, where the defences were weak, thus allowing de Ruyter to claim a major coup. A small group of ships peeled off and entered the Medway, brushed aside the guard ships, broke through the defensive chain and attacked the large ships. These ships were unmanned and disarmed and were easy targets for the Dutch. The *Royal Oak*, *Loyal London* and *Royal James* had been run aground while Albemarle's flagship, *Royal Charles*, was moored and empty of much of its armament.

The Raid on Medway. This audacious attack gave the Dutch the upper hand at the end of the Second Anglo-Dutch War.

The losses were considerable. The diarist, Samuel Pepys, a clerk in the emerging naval administration, received an account of the damage from Edward Gregory, a clerk at Chatham.

> *I'll grapple with a fit of melancholy to answer your expectation. The* Royal Charles *with 32 brass guns in her, and the* Unity *were taken, the* Royal James, Loyal London, Royal Oak, Mathias, Charles V *and* Sancta Maria *were burnt, the* Marmaduke, *five fire ships, two ketches, one fly boat and a dogger sunk … as to the enemy's damage, he had 10 fire ships burned, one man of war … blown up by themselves, and one other great ship burnt also by themselves.*

The English writer John Evelyn observed the tragedy at Chatham for himself and expressed the shock to national pride. 'How triumphantly their whole fleet lay within the very mouth of the Thames … A dreadful spectacle as ever any Englishman saw and a dishonour never to be wiped off.' The Dutch were still in the English Channel when the peace treaty was signed on 31 July 1667 at Breda. The Second Anglo-Dutch War had come to an inglorious end for the English.

THIRD ANGLO-DUTCH WAR

1672-1674

The Third Anglo-Dutch War began when a vainglorious Charles II, needing money, entered a secret scheme with France to crush the Dutch. England would remove the Dutch threat at sea with the Royal Navy, assisted by French ships, while the French took the lead with a land attack on the Dutch by the French army, assisted by a small English contingent. Ostensibly, the war was due to the continued refusal of Dutch warships to recognize the English claim to the Channel and lower their national flag when meeting English warships. On 12 March 1672, Charles ordered an attack on a large Dutch convoy returning from the Mediterranean.

The Dutch navy was still not an easy foe and the Anglo-French combination did help the odds. The English now had 26 articles of war and their fighting instructions. The Dutch had also refined their tactics, and while they did not have general fighting instructions they adopted the line ahead. Before each battle both sides wrote orders of battle for their captains. Both the Dutch and the English navies began to weed out merchant ships from their navies and warship design continued to develop. The four main battles of the Third Anglo-Dutch War comprised the Battle of Sole Bay, the two Battles of Schoonveldt and, in 1673, the Battle of Texel, all of which have been described as confused engagements.

1672 Battle of Sole Bay

The Duke of York's intention, shared by the French commander, Vice Admiral Jean d'Estrées, was to stop the Dutch from gaining access to the North Sea by blockading their ports. At the same time, the Dutch planned to prevent the French and English fleets from combining. Neither side achieved their aims, but the Dutch, in following the allies, managed to surprise them at Sole Bay near Suffolk on 28 May. The French squadron headed south and was engaged in a long-distance fight with a Dutch squadron, while the English and the rest of the Dutch fleet fought it out, with the Dutch having the wind advantage. The Earl of Sandwich was lost, drowned after his ship sank, and the Duke of York had to move his flag from the *Prince*, first to the *St Michael* and then the *London*. The Dutch withdrew in the late afternoon when the wind shifted to the advantage of the English. Both sides claimed victory but the losses were heavy. The English blamed the French and found that the allied composition was a difficult one.

1673 Battles of Schoonveldt

The next year the Dutch and Anglo-French fleets met again in June in the two Battles of Schoonveldt. The Dutch were also defending themselves on the land from a French attack and were only able to pull together a smaller fleet of 64 ships. De Ruyter had planned a second raid on the Medway but this was better defended and he retreated to the mouth of the Scheldt River. Prince Rupert's fleet had 86 ships and he placed the French squadron in the centre while Sir Edward Spragge led the rear. De Ruyter was joined by Admiral Tromp. The numerical superiority of Prince Rupert's fleet was not to their advantage as de Ruyter's position was in a sheltered and shallow area, hindering the

English and French ships. De Ruyter knew the area from childhood and used this knowledge well. Prince Rupert, who has been described as a bold leader but not a sophisticated tactician, had a private battle with Tromp and the allies were forced to withdraw, having gained little. One week later they tried again and once again de Ruyter's tactics held off the superior force and the allies achieved nothing. The French squadron was not effective, and although its position within the fleet was changed, this too was not satisfactory. Admiral d'Estrées and his fellow officers did not understand the English fighting instructions and procedures, and frequently misunderstood tactics or were unsure how to proceed.

Such large fleets and a line of battle extending over 7 miles (11.2 km) meant that communications were a challenge, even in clear visibility. Spragge complained later: 'The Prince placing himself in the van, the French in the middle, the line of battle ... is so very long I cannot see any sign the General Admiral makes.' Rules were drawn up to define the action to be taken in certain situations and the English fighting instructions made it quite clear that the ships were to fight in line and also made clear the priorities in battle. The Dutch fleet's tactics also developed. These were still to grapple and board the opponent, but defensively they began in a line then grouped into twos and threes, providing strength when the English tried to go through the line.

1673 Battle of Texel

On 11 August the fleets met off the island of Texel and the numbers were even more in favour of the allies: 86 to 60. This time the French were in the van and Rupert was in the centre, with Spragge leading the rear squadron. De Ruyter attacked and headed for the centre and Tromp sailed towards Spragge. These two were old enemies and the fight was hard. Spragge was drowned when his barge was hit after moving his flag for the second time. The French, meanwhile, manoeuvred to get the wind advantage and then remained at a safe distance, ignoring Prince Rupert's signals to rejoin the fight. At the end of the battle, de

The Battle of Schoonveldt. Over-extended battle lines, poor tactics and a lack of communication between the Anglo-French allies allowed the Dutch to claim victory in both battles at Schoonveldt.

Ruyter withdrew his fleet without loss after saving his nation from threatened invasion, despite the odds against him. His example of courage and leadership made him a hero to all. The Duke of York admiringly described the Dutch admiral as 'the greatest that ever to that time was in the world'. On 9 February 1674, the English agreed a peace treaty with the Dutch and, just three years later, Charles II's niece, Mary, was married to the Dutch prince, William of Orange. They would later rule England as joint monarchs, after which the two navies combined.

BATTLE OF LA HOGUE

1692

---

*In 1688 King James II fled from London and was
deemed to have effectively abdicated when he threw the
Great Seal of England into the Thames. His Protestant
daughter Mary and her Dutch husband William then
became the first joint rulers of England, following the
'Glorious Revolution'. Aided by the French, James
attempted to regain his throne and invaded Ireland
in March 1689, landing with troops in the south and
later besieging Londonderry. The need to reinforce
and support the troops in Ireland stretched the Royal
Navy, which was short of money and dissatisfied. The
French navy, meanwhile, was in better shape, having
been built up by Colbert, the naval minister to Louis
XIV. Vast sums had been spent to create a fleet of 80
ships of the line, which were generally larger and more
heavily armed than the English fleet.*

William III sailed for Ireland in June 1690 to lead the fight against
James in person. At the same time a large French fleet was heading
up the Channel from Brest. Herbert, Earl of Torrington, despite his
misgivings, was given strict orders to engage with the French. He had
a fleet of 56 ships, including a squadron of Dutch warships, against
the French fleet of 75. The two fleets met off Beachy Head on 30 June

and the French were victorious, although their leader, the Comte de Tourville, was later criticized for not following up his victory more thoroughly. England now saw itself in a perilous situation, with James II in Ireland and a defeated navy, but the following day the good news came that William III had defeated James II's army at the Battle of the Boyne.

James returned to France, but Louis XIV, sensing weakness in England, made plans to invade with an army that would land at Torbay. Seeing themselves as masters of the Channel, the French believed reports that the Royal Navy was largely disaffected with King William. William, however, was planning an invasion of France and his navy was predominantly loyal, even if it had its limitations. The Anglo-Dutch fleet was roughly two-thirds English and one-third Dutch but the commanders-in-chief were always to be English, which was inevitably not popular with the Dutch. Additionally, the Dutch ships were notably slower, which caused difficulties for a combined force operating together.

On 9 May 1692 the commanders of the Anglo-Dutch fleet knew that French naval forces were gathering at La Hogue on the Normandy coast and it was thought they were planning to target the Channel Islands. La Hogue was intended as a large French naval base, and the French military engineer, Vauban, had plans for docks that would allow warships to be moored regardless of tide. He had successfully completed a similar scheme at Dunkirk, but at this stage construction had not yet begun at La Hogue, so any vessel had to be moored off the coast or beached for repairs.

The Anglo-Dutch fleet under the command of Admiral Russell met Tourville's fleet on 19 May. The Dutch squadron was well to the rear of a line that stretched for over 2 miles (3.2 km). The initial engagement was in the centre and Tourville attacked vigorously, hoping that some of the allied ships might defect, but this did not happen. By 4 pm the Dutch and the English centre under Sir Cloudesley Shovell had broken the French line, but the French fleet maintained discipline,

Admiral Russell, commander of the Anglo-Dutch forces at La Hogue. Russell was one of the so-called Immortal Seven, the group of noblemen who issued the invitation to William of Orange in 1688 to depose James II and become England's king.

kept its order and moved westwards. During the night, as fighting ceased, both fleets moved west on the strong tide, but as conditions were foggy the French were able to remain hidden. If the French were well grouped the allies were more scattered, making communication difficult. On 20 May the wind was now to the west and both fleets anchored to effect repairs. They were within just 2 miles of each other. This area has strong flood tides and both commanders knew they had to take maximum advantage of both tide and wind to have any chance of success. One squadron of French ships managed to battle against the westerly wind to go around Cap de la Hague in order to head to Saint-Malo. The rest of the French fleet were caught by a strong front flood tide, which pushed them and the allies back towards Barfleur in the opposite direction. Tourville arrived at Saint-Vaast-la-Hougue with 12 ships, which were in two groups and Russell, with two divisions, now attacked. Using light draught ships that could stay close inshore to stop the French escaping, the allies opened up a preliminary bombardment. As the tide was with them they then sent in a fire ship and six French ships were destroyed. On the morning of 23 May the remaining six French ships were attacked, together with the many transport vessels that were based there to carry the large numbers of troops for the intended invasion. By the end of the day Tourville had lost 12 ships and around 30 transport vessels. Onshore, where over 24,000 French troops were waiting, the losses were witnessed by the exiled King James II and Admiral Tourville, who watched as his flagship, *Soleil Royal*, went up in flames.

The English and the Dutch claimed it as a mighty naval victory, and, even if one French squadron under Pannetier had succeeded in making passage to Saint-Malo, it had lifted the threat of a French invasion. Queen Mary founded the Greenwich naval hospital in celebration. But within a year the French, who had already engaged in a large shipbuilding programme, had replaced all of the ships that were lost. French naval policy now became a *guerre de course* (all French ships were given carte blanche to attack the enemy's merchant fleet),

The Battle of La Hogue. A major historical engagement, La Hogue put an end to France's plans to invade England and restore James II.

and the following year Tourville was avenged when he intercepted a large and valuable convoy estimated at 400 Anglo-Dutch merchant vessels en route to Smyrna. Roughly three-quarters of the convoy escaped but 92 were sunk or captured. The losses were major, equal to the loss sustained from the Great Fire of London in 1666, while the French sold their prizes for 30 million livres – a sum estimated by one distinguished naval historian as equivalent to the French naval budget for one year.

BATTLE OF CAPE PASSARO

1718

In 1717 Spain mobilized its navy and sailed east through the Mediterranean. After successfully taking Sardinia, the fleet with its army on board headed for Sicily, with plans to invade the Italian mainland. This was a direct threat to the delicate balance of peace brokered after the War of the Spanish Succession. The allies, Britain, France and Austria, had tried to ensure that Spain abided by the agreements she had made at the Treaty of Utrecht, which were intended to create a broad basis for European stability. Charles VI, Holy Roman Emperor, had gained the Spanish lands of Lombardy, Sardinia and Naples and this was intensely resented by Philip V of Spain and his Italian wife. Their ambition was to regain the Italian provinces. In order to contain the Spanish, British diplomacy was endeavouring to create a four-power alliance; the traditional enemies France and Britain had combined with the Dutch Republic and they hoped to add Austria.

Britain, France and Austria now urgently needed to stop Spain's actions before a full European war took place and the Royal Navy was deemed most capable of achieving the objective. Accordingly, Admiral Sir George Byng's fleet sailed from England on 20 May 1718. War had not been formally declared and negotiations were continuing. He eventually arrived at Minorca where he learnt of the Spanish plan to organize a league of countries against England and replace George I with the Stuart pretender. The Spanish now had an armada of transports and smaller vessels carrying 16,000 troops and 8,000 cavalry and they arrived on Sicily on 10 July and took the southern part of the island. Byng sought a conference with the Austrian viceroy in Naples and on 15 July the Quadruple Alliance was signed. Byng then headed south to stop the Spanish from taking the rest of Sicily.

Byng was a man of action and decisiveness and, in his view, 'a commanding officer should only call the council of war to screen him from what he has no mind to undertake'. As he reached the narrow Strait of Messina between Sicily and Italy he sent Captain George Saunders to the leader of the Spanish army with a request that they leave the island. This request was refused and Saunders reported that the Spanish seemed to have the intention of attacking the Kingdom of Naples. Byng decided to continue through the strait to attack the Spanish navy.

Just off the south of the island he found the Spanish fleet of 21 warships and associated fire ships and bomb vessels in a line of battle. The Spanish had been unaware of the Royal Navy's movements or indeed of the ongoing diplomatic activity. They then moved away, still in line of battle, followed through the night by Byng and by the next morning he had nearly caught up with them. Many of the Spanish warships were lightly built, having been designed by Admiral Antonio Gaztañeta as streamlined warships whose main purpose was to protect merchant ships rather than to form a line of battle.

Admiral Byng's fleet at Naples. The Royal Navy's ships stopped off en route to Sicily so that the Quadruple Alliance could be formally signed.

Initially a small breakaway group of six Spanish warships, together with the galleys, fire ships and bomb ships, separated from the main Spanish fleet and moved towards the shore, pursued by Captain George Walton on the *Canterbury*, together with five other ships. The rest of the British fleet then engaged with the Spanish. Rather than forming a line of battle, Byng's ships pursued them in a general chase, with the result that his captains engaged ships of a similar size and approached on either side of the Spanish line. The first two ships, *Grafton* and *Orford*, did not open fire until the stern guns of the rear Spanish ship had been used to attack them. The British then returned fire and captured the *Santa Rosa*. Subsequent British ships were also successful and by 1 pm the *Kent* and the *Grafton* had engaged Admiral Gaztañeta's flagship. Byng, on the *Barfleur*, was astern but Captain Streynsham Master, Byng's brother-in-law, took the honours in his 60-gun ship, *Superb*, and captured the Spanish commander-in-chief as his prisoner of war. The rest of the Spanish fleet were successfully engaged, including two Spanish ships commanded by a former captain in the Royal Navy, Rear Admiral George Camocke, who had been dismissed in 1714 for supporting the Stuart cause.

At the end of the day Byng's fleet had captured 11 ships and destroyed three more of the 21-strong Spanish fleet, putting an end to Spain's ambitions to create a wider European league against Britain. However, it took rather longer to persuade the Spanish to relinquish Sicily. It was only after two more years of military persuasion, including a blockade of Sicily's ports plus a French invasion of Spain, that the Spanish withdrew from Italy. Admiral Byng remained in the Mediterranean, playing a leading role in diplomatic efforts and the Franco-British alliance lasted until 1731.

BATTLE OF CAPE FINISTERRE

1747

Thirty years after the Battle of Cape Passaro, Britain, France and Spain were rivals for overseas trade and colonial empires. In North America and India, the British and the French were in a power struggle. The priority for the Royal Navy was the protection of trade and the prevention of French reinforcements getting to their overseas bases. Rear Admiral George Anson was appointed to command the Western Squadron in August 1746, which would protect trade, harass the enemy and cruise as an anti-invasion force. Anson, famous for his circumnavigation of the world between 1740 and 1744, was guarding the entrance to the English Channel.

The French were targeting India and had captured Madras in 1746, but they needed reinforcements to consolidate their position and take over British factories. So, 18 merchant ships from the French East India company, escorted by three warships, were sent from Rochefort in the spring of 1747. Due to gales they were unable to get very far and fell in at Aix Roads with another French convoy of 24 merchant vessels heading for Canada. This convoy was escorted by five warships under the command of Rear Admiral de la Jonquière. The combined force decided to sail together to Madeira and by 2 May they had reached a point 12 miles (19 km) north of Cape Finisterre.

Such a large group of well-armed merchant ships and their warship protectors could not go unnoticed and Anson was already searching for them. First he headed south to the Bay of Biscay, ensuring that the men on board all of his ships were in a state of battle readiness. Then he formed a line of his ships, keeping them almost a mile apart from each other to create a sweeping barrier to catch the French fleet. By the morning of 3 May he was notified of the large enemy force ahead.

Anson had more ships and guns than the French, including 14 ships of the line, among which was his 90-gun flagship, the *Prince George*, nine ships of at least 60 guns and two 50-gun gunships. The French admiral saw the British begin to chase and placed himself between their ships and his merchant convoy. He then formed a line of battle with his warships and three of the large East India ships. The British ships were in a line ahead, with Captain Boscawen leading in HMS *Namur*. Discipline at this stage was crucial, as the line of battle gained its main strength from its unity and combined firepower. Rear Admiral Peter Warren in HMS *Devonshire* was second-in-command to Anson and was anxious to get at the convoy to prevent it escaping. But as he attempted to speed up towards the French he was quickly recalled to his proper position.

By the early afternoon Anson had sent his leading ships towards the centre of the French line, which caused two of the French East Indiamen to panic and move out of their line. Seeing that his attempted line of battle was falling apart Jonquière signalled a retreat and Anson then gave the order for a general chase. Freed from the restrictions of the line there was a rush to claim prizes and at 4 pm Captain Dennis in the 50-gun *Centurion* was the first to directly encounter the French. As more British ships came up using their very effective and accurate gunnery, they captured several French ships. A contemporary account of the battle noted the jealous competition between the British

Vice Admiral George Anson, commander of British forces at Cape Finisterre. A very capable military leader, he was also an excellent administrator and introduced many reforms and efficiencies into the Royal Navy.

commanders for the various prizes. In total they took six men-of-war and several East Indiamen, plus five merchant ships and three frigates. Anson was impressed by the gallantry of the French, but was very pleased with the results of the training he had imposed on his squadron on the way to the battle. In his view the victory was a credit to British gunnery.

> *The fire on our side was much greater and more regular than theirs; and it is evident our shott were better plac'd …They behaved all very well and lost their ships with honour and reputation, but I can without vanity say that our ships were better disciplined and made much hotter fire upon them, than they did upon us, and it was easy to judge whose fire was best before the gross of my fleet got up, and they were superior in strength to my ships that engaged them.*

The welcome news was sent back to Britain on the *Centurion* with Captain Dennis, who received £500 as a reward. Anson gained a peerage and was enriched by the considerable prize money and four years later he became First Lord of the Admiralty. The *Invincible*, which was captured at Finisterre, was just three years old and, as a 74-gun ship, was a new design by French naval architects. Now added to the Royal Navy, it was closely examined and used as a model for future warships. Strategically, the battle known as the Battle of Cape Ortegal to the French had wider implications. The French naval strength was damaged and the reinforcements needed for both Canada and India did not arrive, weakening the French position there. The lesson in fighting tactics demonstrated that a well-trained and unified squadron could prevail and victories could be gained by taking calculated risks and being flexible, rather than sticking strictly to standard tactics.

BATTLE OF QUIBERON BAY

1759

From 1739 until 1815 Britain and France would be at war almost continuously. The Seven Years' War, which began in 1756, involved all of the great European powers, but in North America it took the form of a battle for domination between the French and the British. In the first place, this was largely a consequence of friction between French and British settlers in North America. The Battle of Quiberon Bay has been described as one of the finest and most important victories in the long history of the Royal Navy. It was fought in a gale in the shallows of a dangerous rocky coast and victory was the result of a feat of great seamanship, not just gunpower.

To distract British efforts in North America, the French decided to invade Britain and began building up their fleet. The French naval forces were scattered, however, as the Marquis de Conflans was in Brest with 21 warships and 12 more were based in the Mediterranean in the Toulon squadron. Meanwhile, French troops were assembling at Vannes in Brittany and at Ostend. Knowing the French fleet needed to escape from its confinement in Brest, the British maintained a blockade and sent Admiral Sir Edward Hawke in May 1759 to increase its effectiveness.

The blockade was logistically difficult and frequently caused severe health problems for the men on board due to a lack of fresh supplies. It speaks volumes for Admiral Hawke's management that he succeeded in keeping a significant fleet of at least 32 ships of the line at sea for over six months. By setting up a regular supply system, with transports bringing out live cattle, vegetables and beer from Plymouth to the blockade, Hawke kept his ships and the men on the ships healthy throughout both the summer and the autumn. James Lind, a naval physician, was amazed:

> *It is an observation, I think, worthy of record that 14,000 persons, pent up in ships, should continue, the six or seven months, to enjoy a better state of health upon the watery element, then it can well be imagined so great a number of people would enjoy, on the most healthful spot of ground in the world.*

Regular training was essential to keep the men effective and busy. The possibility of a battle between two large fleets had Hawke impressing on his captains the importance of very close engagement. While the fighting instructions largely emphasized the standard line of battle, Hawke preferred to chase the enemy. However, they could not maintain their station at all times and it was not the health of his men but the weather conditions that forced him to move away from Brest on several occasions.

Westerly gales in November caused the British fleet to take refuge in Torbay, and on 16 November Hawke heard that the French fleet had slipped out of port. Despite gale force winds, Hawke set out in pursuit and a few days later he saw the French heading into Quiberon Bay, in Brittany. The French had 21 ships and Hawke had 23 ships of the line. The French were suffering from a shortage of men and a third of them were inexperienced seamen, while the British fleet had been continually at sea while training its crews. The French commander mistakenly thought he had more time and believed that the British would not risk heading into the unknown and rocky waters of Quiberon Bay in fading light and with a severe gale. Despite the dangers, Hawke was determined to continue his pursuit and simply followed the route taken by the French, effectively using them as pilots. By mid-afternoon, the British had caught up with the French fleet and Hawke ordered a general engagement.

There was a wind shift to the disadvantage of the French but the navigational risks to the British were still very high. Conflans, the French commander, was targeted by Hawke and in the ensuing battle

Richard Wright's painting Battle of Quiberon Bay: the Day After *(1760) is a symbolic representation of the literal and figurative shipwreck of France's military ambitions in North America.*

he was unable to escape. A fierce battle was fought in heavy seas and in the morning light came the reckoning. In total, the French lost seven ships of the line. Conflans' flagship was one of six wrecked or sunk, another being captured, and the British lost just two ships but rescued their crews. The Brest fleet had been largely destroyed and it rounded off a year of victories for the British.

Much of the success can be attributed to Hawke, who has been described as a British commanding admiral of exceptional calibre with a 'very cool head and a fund of moral and physical courage'. In his report, Hawke noted the loss of two ships and commented:

The hard gales on the day of action, flying enemy, the shortness of the day, on the coast we are on, I can boldly affirm that all that could possibly be done has been done. As to the loss we have sustained, let it be placed in account of the necessity I was under running all risks to break the strong force of the enemy.

He was decisive and aggressive despite the weather conditions and navigational risks and his dramatic defeat of the French fleet disabled it as a fighting force. The French navy was demoralized. Captain Bigot of the *Magnifique* wrote: 'I do not know everything about it, but I know too much. The battle of the 20th has annihilated the Navy and finished its plans.'

BATTLE OF FLAMBOROUGH HEAD

1779

John Paul Jones enjoys major status as one of America's great naval heroes, but his greatest achievement received comparatively little recognition at the time. During the American War of Independence the American navy was very limited in size and scope and much of its activity at sea involved privateers: privately owned vessels with the authority to attack enemy merchant vessels. Privateering was an opportunist's game and John Paul Jones was very much the opportunist and a lone actor. He is described by one of his biographers as 'tough, impatient, self absorbed, aggressive and charming', with a determination to advance economically and socially. He had pursued a varied and controversial career since leaving Scotland, his place of birth, and by 1775 he had used his connections to become a lieutenant in the nascent US Navy. The navy had few large warships and used its smaller, faster vessels to attack merchant shipping, in which Jones was very successful.

When France entered the war as allies of the United States, Jones sailed from Virginia in 1777 in an 18-gun sloop, the *Ranger*, claiming two prize ships on the way. After reaching Nantes he spent some time in Paris, pressing for a larger ship and more assistance from the French. Then, in spring 1778, still with his sloop *Ranger*, he set off for the Irish Sea. In northwest England, an area he knew well from his early life, he boldly raided the coast, including landing at Whitehaven and setting fire to the old fort. Among his prizes was the capture of a small 20-gun British frigate, HMS *Drake*. This caused a considerable stir in the British news, annoyed the government and delighted the French, who rewarded him with a larger ship, a 900-ton East Indiaman which Jones renamed the *Bonhomme Richard*.

Jones then set out to lead a diversionary attack on British shipping to assist the Franco-Spanish fleet in the English Channel. His squadron was not part of the official French navy but it included the 36-gun frigate *Alliance*, the 32-gun *Pallas* and the 12-gun *Vengeance*, all of which were owned by the French king. Jones led his squadron around Britain and Ireland, capturing many prizes, and at one stage tried to demand a ransom from Leith, the port of Edinburgh, but was driven off by poor weather. On 20 September, heading south, Jones's squadron met a large convoy of ships from the Baltic just off the East Coast, escorted by two British warships: *Countess of Scarborough* with 20 guns and the frigate *Serapis* with 44 guns. The Royal Navy escorts enabled the merchant ships to scatter and escape and then turned towards Jones's squadron.

Jones should have had the immediate advantage with his four ships, but the small *Vengeance* avoided conflict and the *Alliance* had a rather eccentric Frenchman, Pierre Landais, as its captain. The battle was hard fought as the *Serapis* and the *Bonhomme Richard* went head-to-head and the latter opened fire. An explosion occurred when two of the 18-pounder guns on the *Bonhomme Richard* burst and, meanwhile, the 30-gun *Pallas* captured the *Countess of Scarborough*. In the fight between the *Serapis* and the *Bonhomme Richard* the larger

John Paul Jones. The Scots-born naval commander is often referred to as 'the father of the American Navy', due to his daring conduct in war. His larger-than-life, forceful personality won him as many enemies as friends in his adopted homeland of America, and, unable to secure a regular command after the Revolutionary Wars he joined the Imperial Russian Navy as a Rear Admiral.

British ship with the better-trained crew seemed to be in the ascendant. Captain Pearson of the *Serapis* tried to cut across the bows of his assailant in an attempt to rake fire down the deck, while Jones drove his bows into the stern of the *Serapis*, trying to board the larger ship. As the two ships fired at close quarters and a shell hit the American flag, Pearson shouted across, 'Has your ship struck?', assuming they were about to surrender. This led to one of the most famous sayings in American history as Jones defiantly replied, 'I have not yet begun to fight!', even as his ship was at risk of sinking beneath him.

The two fought on, and when a grenade was thrown into an open hatch on the *Serapis*, exploding and killing 20 sailors, the tide turned. The *Alliance*, which until now had not been much in evidence, headed towards the *Bonhomme Richard* to assist and Pearson of the *Serapis* surrendered. However, in the confusion of battle the *Alliance* accidentally shot the *Bonhomme Richard* and John Paul Jones later wrongly accused the French captain of trying to aid *Serapis*. The squadron took its prizes but the *Bonhomme Richard* had to be abandoned. Jones then took the *Serapis* and sailed triumphantly into Amsterdam, where he was warmly welcomed, but he had to leave and head for Lorient after a protest from the British ambassador to the Netherlands. The prisoners were handed to the French and the *Serapis* was later acquired by King Louis.

This capture of the two British warships was a significant morale boost for the Americans and served to increase the fame of John Paul Jones in Europe. The French awarded him honours and he was welcomed by great crowds. In America, an almost bankrupt Congress could do little but give him a vote of thanks and the command of another ship. But by the time his ship was ready for sea the war was almost at an end. American historians note him as a superb and highly skilled handler of ships, 'but too inexperienced and arrogant to be an effective squadron commander'. Jones did not get another command, although he did serve for a time in the Russian navy. He died in Paris in 1792.

BATTLE OF CHESAPEAKE BAY

1781

Chesapeake Bay is an excellent example of a naval battle that was not exactly a clear win or an outright victory for either side, but where the consequences on land were major. America's allies, in the fight for independence, fought off a British fleet and the result led to the defeat of British forces on land. Thus the French navy and its allies, the navies of Spain and the Netherlands, made a vital contribution to American independence.

At this time, the Americans had no real navy of their own and little experience in building warships as the Royal Navy preferred to have warships built in its own yards, or in private yards where they could be closely supervised. The American colonies, however, excelled in privateers, built for speed and used for capturing enemy merchant ships. Hundreds had been used in the War of Jenkins' Ear and in the Seven Years' War. But they were short of naval armament, and then there was the problem of manning the ships. Most Americans served on merchant vessels and while they could adapt quickly to life on a warship there were very few experienced naval officers to lead them. The support of the French navy and other allies was therefore crucial.

French support for the Americans involved several strands. They provided troop transport to help bolster Washington's numbers and their navy was fighting the British in the West Indies. The French were determined to win back territory there and it also served to keep some of the Royal Navy occupied in that area. Admiral de Grasse left France for the West Indies in March 1781 with a good sized fleet of 20 line of battle ships, frigates, transport and supply ships. Meanwhile General Rochambeau had landed a French expeditionary force at Newport.

In the West Indies, Grasse successfully captured St Lucia and then headed for Haiti to collect more troops to reinforce Rochambeau. In America, the British Army under Cornwallis was heading through Carolina and Virginia towards Chesapeake Bay, while General Rochambeau was coming from the north to join the Continental Army, led by George Washington. Both sides wanted to secure access to the coast for supplies so Grasse decided to head for Hampton Roads at the mouth of the Chesapeake to give support to the combined army.

The British squadron in the West Indies was commanded by Rear Admiral Sir Samuel Hood. Hurricane season was approaching in the West Indies so Admiral Rodney sent Hood with ten ships of the line to reinforce North America and find Grasse and his squadron. Hood tried to pre-empt Grasse by arriving ahead of him in Hampton Roads, but finding it deserted he headed towards the Hudson, where he met up with the more senior Rear Admiral Thomas Graves and his fleet. The French fleet headed by Grasse subsequently arrived at Hampton Roads and, unimpeded, landed the extra troops for Washington.

Cornwallis, meanwhile, had fortified Yorktown and was expecting the Royal Navy to meet him. Aware that the Continental Army was on the move to Virginia, Graves and Hood sailed from the Hudson in support of the British troops at Yorktown. They were concerned that the French squadron off Rhode Island, under the command of Rear Admiral Comte Barras de St Laurent, would meet up with Grasse in the Chesapeake.

When they arrived they had the upper hand as the French were not expecting them. When the British sails were sighted and it was announced that there were at least 20 men of war, Grasse rushed his ships out of the narrow channel into the bay. It was at this point that Graves made a tactical error by allowing the ships of the French squadron to come out and form a line of battle, rather than attacking them individually. The fighting instructions of the Admiralty were too rigid for this situation and communication was confused between the ships of the British fleet. Despite arriving at 10 am with all the advantage of surprise, it was not until 4 pm that action truly began, with the French putting up a strong fight. It required initiative and tactical flexibility, which was not much in evidence from Hood, and much of the fighting was left to Graves. The French casualties amounted to 220, the British to 336, and the British vessels were disproportionately damaged. Just two of the French ships had suffered serious damage while five of the British ships were in a serious state, one having to be abandoned.

It was a confused encounter and the French were able to return to the Chesapeake while Graves and Hood went back to New York to repair their ships. Barras and his fleet carrying the French army siege train safely reached the Chesapeake, so Grasse now had 36 warships. With control of that coastline, Washington and Rochambeau targeted Yorktown and Cornwallis capitulated there on 19 October. The triumph of the French navy over the British at the Battle of Chesapeake Bay led to the fall of Yorktown and saved the United States from economic collapse. Within the Royal Navy the recriminations began, with Hood citing Graves' poor signalling as the reason why his ships had not come into close action, while Graves shouldered the full responsibility. Admiral Rodney blamed everyone and falsely claimed he had seen it coming.

BATTLE OF THE SAINTES

1782

One year after the inconclusive naval Battle of Chesapeake Bay precipitated the loss of Yorktown, the French Admiral de Grasse and the British Admiral Rodney met in another more decisive battle. This time it was in the West Indies and included all the senior officers who had met at Chesapeake. Grasse, Barras, Graves and Hood had returned to their relative stations in November 1781.

Hood, who was seen as limited in his response in the previous battle, made up for it with a clever use of tactics and disciplined seamanship at St Kitts. The French navy had assisted a landing of French troops to take St Kitts and, on 25 January, Hood attempted to rescue the beleaguered British garrison. He lured Grasse out of his anchorage then slipped in behind him and anchored close to the shore to keep the French at bay. However, with few land troops there was little Hood could do to assist onshore and his fleet of 22 ships was underpowered against a French force of 30 ships. When the British garrison fell, his ships were then in severe danger, being caught between the French on land and at sea. However, at 11 pm, by a prearranged and carefully coordinated action, each British ship cut its anchor and silently sailed out and in the morning the French found an empty bay.

The French continued with their territorial plans and Jamaica was a key target, as capturing that wealthy island would hurt Britain both economically and strategically. Grasse had 34 ships of the line and on 8 April they were escorting a convoy of transport ships carrying 10,000 troops from Fort Royal, the French naval base at Martinique. His plan was to meet up with the Spanish to attack Jamaica, but this was foiled when they were pursued by 36 ships of the line of the British fleet, led by Admirals Rodney and Samuel Hood, who left from St Lucia. This led to the engagement known as the Battle of the Saintes being fought over an expanse of sea that lay between the islands of Dominica and Guadeloupe.

In the early morning of 12 April 1782 the two fleets were just four or five leagues distant from each other. The *Marlborough,* captained by Taylor Penny, opened fire at 8 am and at this point the fleets were formed up in line of battle, with the French heading south and the British heading north while firing at one another. The winds were variable and light, which caused difficulties in tactics for both navies. However, slowing progress by backing the topsails enabled a lengthy exchange of fire between the *Ville de Paris*, flagship of Grasse, and Rodney's flagship, the *Formidable*, which was in the centre of the line. The problem with gunfire was the vast amount of smoke produced, which made visibility poor as the light winds were insufficient to lift the haze it created.

By 9 am a change of wind was causing the French fleet difficulties in keeping its course. There was a series of collisions and the British had the benefit. The *Glorieux*'s masts were destroyed by fire from the *Canada* and the heavy masts fell over the side, causing the ship to roll with her gun ports under the sea. Rodney then broke through the French lines, enabling him to rake four of the French ships. He was followed by the *Namur*, the *St Albans*, the *Canada*, the *Repulse* and the *Ajax*. Commodore Affleck's ship, the *Bedford*, similarly caused division with a third break of the French line. It has been argued that this breaking of the line was a highly significant tactic, later to

The Battle of the Saintes. This was Britain's most significant victory over France during the American Revolutionary War.

be brilliantly used by Nelson, but it was not a planned move. It was unintentional, due to the winds, and in the end not wholly successful. Rodney had set out to destroy the French fleet but, while Grasse's flagship was cut off, much of the French fleet was able to escape.

By 9.30 am the French were in several disorganized groups and casualties were high, particularly in the transport ships carrying so many troops. An abstract from the log of the British ship *Barfleur*, indicates the slow-motion effect of the light winds.

> *... forty five past ten the* Barfleur *ceased firing, the enemy's last ships having passed her. Light airs incline aboard to calms. Hoisted out two boats to tow the ship's head towards the enemy. When the smoke cleared away saw the enemy's fleet lowered and ours standing towards them. Got the ship's head towards the enemy. Employed refitting the rigging and making all the sail we could.*

Rodney gathered his fleet and attacked again in the afternoon, initially maintaining a line of battle but then releasing each ship to 'annoy the enemy as their respective commanders judge best'. By mid-afternoon the British had taken many prizes, of which the greatest was the French flagship, the 110-gun *Ville de Paris*. Further French ships were taken a week later. In total, Rodney's fleet captured seven ships of the line. Rodney was particularly pleased by the capture of the *Ardent* as she was carrying the French siege train designed for use against Jamaica. Rodney's victory reversed the tide of war but he was subsequently criticized by Samuel Hood, his second-in-command, for not following up his victory.

Celebrations were extensive when the news reached London on 18 May and there were bonfires and fireworks in towns across Britain. Rodney's image was soon seen on pottery mugs and teapots. The saving of Jamaica was particularly celebrated as its loss would not just have been a fiscal blow but also psychological. Saintes was a very welcome victory after a succession of failures since the fall of Yorktown and Britain could reburnish its tarnished military and naval reputation amongst the European powers. Furthermore, it put Britain in a position of strength to negotiate the general peace that followed.

BATTLE OF THE GLORIOUS FIRST OF JUNE

1794

In the early years of the French Revolution there were severe problems with the grain harvests and parts of France were almost in the famine stage, so the Directorate was forced to import large amounts of grain from America. In 1794, a fleet of 117 vessels sailed from Chesapeake Bay carrying colonial goods and the vital grain, with a small convoy escort under Rear Admiral Vanstabel. The French home fleet was on the alert to cover the arrival of the convoy and, indeed, Rear Admiral Louis Thomas Villaret-Joyeuse had on board a senior delegate from the Jacobin government to ensure his loyalty and dedication to the task.

The British, meanwhile, were also at sea under Lord Howe to provide cover for an outward-bound convoy. When they reached the Lizard, Howe detached Rear Admiral Montagu to defend the British convoy as far as Cape Finisterre and also sent Captain Peter Rainier with a small group of ships to look after the convoy further into the Atlantic. Howe now had just 26 ships of the line, seven frigates, one hospital ship and two fireships. This was about the same size as the French fleet under Villaret, who was under orders not to engage the British unless the vital convoy was at risk of not reaching its destination.

The conditions were so foggy that the enemy fleets actually passed one another on 17 May and did not fully see each other until 28 May. There was then a brief skirmish when a small number of British ships attacked the rear of the French and the French sustained a loss of 400 men. The next day the fleets remained within sight of each other and the British endeavoured to get to the favoured windward side of the French. Tactics and signalling had been developed since the American war. Howe believed in a centralized command system, limiting the captains' initiative, and he had also rewritten the signal book and fighting instructions. The coming battle was an opportunity to test his new signals and tactics. Some years later, Admiral the Earl of St Vincent wrote a description of the battle: 'On 29 May a manoeuvre by which Lord Howe proposed to cut off the rear of the enemy, by passing through his line, failed in effect, owing to the mistake or disobedience of signals; the only advantage gained was the weather gage.'

Howe had supplemented signals with messages sent by frigates but his captains had not fully understood his tactics. However, having gained the favourable position Howe now considered his next tactics against the French, who were maintaining a line ahead, and at 7.25 am he ordered his ships to attack. St Vincent later described the action as Howe led his ships in his flagship, *Queen Charlotte*:

> *He ran down in a line abreast, nearly at right angles with enemy's line, until he brought every ship of his fleet on a diagonal point of bearing to the opponent, then steering on an angle to preserve that bearing until he arrived on the weather quarter, and close to the centre ship of the enemy, when the* Queen Charlotte *altered her course, and steered at right angles through the enemy's line, raking their ships on both sides as she crossed, and then luffing up and engaging to leeward.*

Glorious First of June. This was the first and largest sea battle between Britain and France in the Revolutionary Wars.

The main engagement began at 9.24 am and the British used their superior rate of fire to good effect, although not all of the British ships were successful in passing through and were forced to fight on the windward. By the end of the fierce fighting one French ship was sunk and six more were captured. By 6.15 pm Villaret had withdrawn what was left of his fleet.

Howe was in no position to finish the French as the rigging and masts of the British ships were badly damaged in the battle, so they limped home, eventually arriving at Spithead on 13 June. In the British fleet 290 men were killed and 858 wounded. The French losses were enormous: 4,200 men were killed or wounded and 3,300 were taken prisoner. It was the heaviest loss suffered by the French Navy since 1692. Collingwood later admiringly described the French as having fought with 'savage ferocity'. But the French had achieved their objective and saved the convoy, which was to be the cause of much celebration in France, while the British celebrated a major early win in the wars. It has been described as the last of the traditional eighteenth century ship engagements, but it gave rise to tactics that would be honed in the coming years. This battle also had an unusual name, as most sea battles are named after the nearest piece of land and this one was simply named after the date of most of the action, as it was fought so far out in the Atlantic.

BATTLE OF CAPE ST VINCENT

1797

Cape St Vincent was not noted for the large number of ships captured, just four, and might in some terms be considered less important than many other battles. However, it came at a time when Britain badly needed a victory and the commander of the Mediterranean Fleet, Admiral Sir John Jervis, was showered with high honours. He was given the titles of Baron Jervis of Meaford, the place of his birth, and Earl of St Vincent, and received a pension of £3,000 a year for life and a sword and a gold medal from the king. It was also a battle that showcased the brilliance of an officer, Horatio Nelson, even if his action that day was controversial.

It was a morale boost at a time when Britain was at a low ebb. The war with France had been ongoing since 1793, campaigns in the West Indies were not going well and deaths from disease were mounting. Spain allied itself with France and declared war on Britain in 1796, France drew up invasion plans and in the Mediterranean many ports were now closed to the British. On 22 February 1797, three French frigates landed 1,500 troops near Fishguard in Wales. While the incursion into Wales collapsed without a shot being fired, the impact on the British public was severe, causing a run on the banks. This threatened an acute financial crisis just as funds were needed to prosecute the war with France.

Jervis was the son of a barrister and, rather than go into law as he was destined, he ran away to join the navy aged 14. He made steady progress and in 1778 he was described by Lord Sandwich as, 'a good officer, but turbulent and busy'. In 1796 he was in command of the Mediterranean fleet when the combined Franco-Spanish fleet sailed out of Toulon. The French headed for Lorient but the Spanish needed to refit and put into Cartagena. Tasked with escorting four ships carrying mercury, an essential item for use in Spain's American silver mines, the Spanish fleet sailed on 1 February 1797, heading for Cádiz. The fleet was inexperienced, undermanned and short of supplies, while the British fleet of 15 ships, on the other hand, was in a much better state and was commanded by a respected admiral. Nelson had high regard for Jervis and his leadership qualities, writing in 1796, 'They at home do not know what this fleet is capable of performing; anything and everything … of all the fleets I ever saw, I never saw one, in point of officers and men equal to Sir John Jervis's, who is a commander able to lead them to glory.'

Nelson's words reflect the efficiency and high morale of the fleet. Jervis was on his flagship, the 100-gun *Victory*, and they were cruising off the coast of Spain when Jervis was informed of the Spanish squadron. It was foggy and, as they loomed out of the mist, one British lookout exclaimed: 'By my soul they are thumpers!' He was right. Among the Spanish ships was the *Santísima Trinidad*, a first-rate ship of the line with four decks and probably the largest ship in the world at that time. Three of the Spanish ships had more than 100 guns on board.

As they were counted and the figure reached 27, nearly double the British fleet, Jervis exclaimed: 'The die is cast and if there are fifty sail I will go through them!' Despite the odds the British fleet

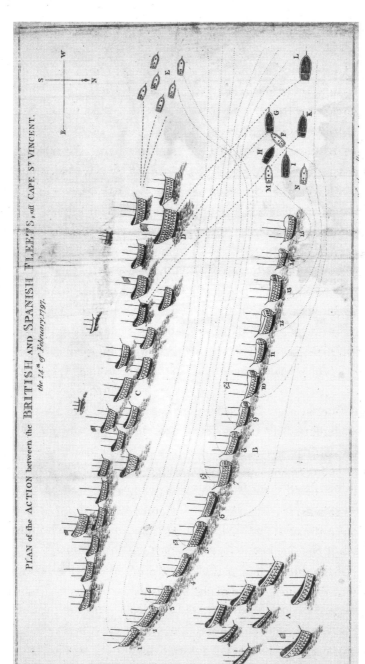

A contemporary plan of the action at Cape St Vincent.

prepared their ships for war, clearing gun decks and forming battle lines. Towards the rear was the 74-gun *Captain*, commanded by Commodore Horatio Nelson.

The Spanish also prepared themselves and attempted to unite in the classic line of battle. Their fleet was in two sections, with 18 warships and one transport to windward and the other five ships of the line escorting the remaining four transports to leeward. Seeing a gap between them, Jervis went through and then turned to attack from the rear. The Spanish counter-attacked and Jervis sent a signal to Sir Charles Thompson's division in the rear, among them Nelson in the *Captain*, to take up a suitable station and get into action as soon as possible. Naval signals were not sufficiently precise for Jervis to explain exactly what he intended and some of his rearmost ships did not respond. But Nelson had noticed the leading Spanish ships moving as though to attack the British rear. Without direct orders, Nelson speedily took his ship out of the line and headed for the rapidly closing gap, placing his vessel and his men in great danger. Jervis was quick to see what was happening and sent two more ships to follow Nelson.

The Spaniards abandoned their move towards the British rear and headed north-west, their line disintegrating as they went. By 2 pm the fight was at its height as the British ships overtook and engaged the Spaniards. Nelson's first attack had caused so much smoke that the Spanish ships risked firing at each other when they fired back. Two badly damaged ships, the *San Nicolás* and the *San Josef*, collided. Nelson's ship was then disabled and he took a rare decision not just to board the *San Nicolás* but to lead the boarding party himself. He and his men took the *San Nicolás* and the *San Josef*, while others captured the *Salvador del Mundo* and the *San Ysidro*.

At around 4.30 pm Jervis gave the signal to break off the action. The Spaniards had lost four ships, four others were badly damaged and it was impossible for them to renew the action, so they decided to sail away. The flagship *Santísima Trinidad* had been dismasted and

Admiral Córdoba moved to a frigate. Several British ships attempted to take the *Santísima Trinidad*, which with four decks would have been a magnificent prize, but it was towed off by another Spanish ship. Jervis, however, had gained complete victory, taking four prizes from a greatly superior enemy. The British fleet, guarding its prizes, made first for Lagos on 16 February for immediate repairs and then for Lisbon, where they arrived on 24 February. Seventy-three men of the British fleet had been killed, of whom 24 came from Nelson's ship.

News of the victory, which reached London on 3 March, was greeted with delighted relief. After the bad news of the preceding months and the general fear of invasion, a victory at sea over the Spanish was a cause for great celebration. Nelson made sure that his name was not forgotten and the public were enthusiastic about his conspicuous heroism in personally leading a boarding party, even if some of his fellow officers were less impressed at such self-seeking behaviour. As a result of the battle, Nelson got his knighthood and the Spanish fleet became reluctant to put to sea.

BATTLE OF CAMPERDOWN

1797

France conquered the United Provinces in 1793, renaming it the Batavian Republic, taking the Dutch fleet under its control. The British were alert to any signs of French invasion and Admiral Duncan had the task of blockading the Dutch fleet in the Texel. But in March 1797 there was a naval mutiny at Spithead and then another at Nore on 12 May. This left Duncan to keep up the pretence of a blockade with just two ships. After the mutinies were resolved it left a badly shaken command system with many officers concerned for their own safety.

In October, Admiral Duncan went into Yarmouth to refit his flagship and take on stores. While there, he discovered that the Dutch fleet commanded by Vice Admiral de Winter was at sea. De Winter had orders to engage the enemy and draw them towards the Dutch coastline if possible and he was off the coastal village of Kamperduin (Camperdown) heading back to port when he was seen by Duncan's fleet. The British ships were larger and the waters there were very shallow – as the Dutch well knew – but Duncan decided to press an attack. The two enemies were evenly matched, with 16 battleships each, a mixture of 74-gun ships and some 64- and 50-gun ships.

Captain Trollope's squadron sighted the Dutch at 9 am and signalled to Duncan who immediately made the signal for a general chase. The Dutch formed a line between the British and the shallow coastline. Later, Duncan in his own words described the initial action:

> *Finding there was no time to be lost in making the attack, I made the signal to bear up, break the enemy's line and engage them to leeward, each ship her opponent, by which I got between them and the land, which they were fast approaching.*

Only some of his ships were able fully to interpret his signal. Signalling then was at an early stage of development and some ships had out of date signals. With his two divisions, Duncan attacked the rear and another division headed for the centre of the Dutch line, passed through and then attacked them from the other side. The action began around 12.30 pm and was two-and-a-half hours of hard fighting, as Duncan led his division towards the centre and the Dutch commander-in-chief. Duncan observed that de Winter's flagship, *Vrijheid,* despite being 'defended for some time in a most gallant manner... being oppressed by numbers, her colours were struck.'

The Admiral was brought on board Duncan's flagship, the *Venerable.* As was the custom, Admiral de Winter offered his sword to Admiral Duncan, who refused it, saying, 'I would much rather take a brave man's hand than his sword.' De Winter later told Duncan that '[Your] not waiting to form line ruined me. If I had got nearer the shore and you had attacked, I should properly have drawn both fleets onto it, it would mean a victory for me, being on my own coast.'

Shortly afterwards, a second Dutch Vice Admiral also struck his flag. Now would be the time to complete the action, but the large British ships were getting close to the shore and in shallow water and the wind was blowing them onto the land. The British managed to take eight ships as prizes, but overnight several of the Dutch vessels were able to slip away into the Texel. The prizes were heavily damaged and two sank before they could be got back to Britain and none of them could be taken into the fleet.

In this battle there is a rare occasion when the presence of a woman on board is mentioned. Women, usually wives of the men on board, are known to have gone to sea, but as they were never on the official muster roll, they occur only in very rare sightings such as this letter from an officer on HMS *Ardent* at the Battle of Camperdown. His words seem remarkably matter of fact:

Our wounded are in general dreadfully mangled. One of the men's wives assisted in firing a gun where her husband was quartered, though frequently requested to go below, but she would not be prevailed on to do so until a shot carried away one of her legs and wounded the other.

The listed British casualties, which are unlikely to have included the gunner's wife, were 240 killed and 796 wounded. The Dutch lost 540 killed and 620 wounded. The Battles of both Cape St Vincent and Camperdown meant that the French invasion plans were now over. In the words of naval historian, Professor Nicholas Rodger, 'The British had never won a victory remotely equivalent against more or less equal forces.'

BATTLE OF THE NILE

1798

---

*In 1798, 39-year-old Rear Admiral Horatio Nelson
was in the Mediterranean seeking the French fleet.
He had command of his own fleet for the first time
and a clear target. Napoleon had persuaded his
superiors to permit him to take an expedition to
Egypt. His plan was to take Egypt and then use it
as a base from which to tackle India, which would
strike a decisive blow against Britain. Apart from
gaining the riches of India he could potentially cut
off the only supply of saltpetre, an essential item
in gunpowder. The French fleet was supporting
over 100 transport vessels, which were carrying
Bonaparte's army. They had successfully taken
Malta and had then landed in Egypt, where they had
won a decisive battle against local troops in July.
Britain was largely oblivious to this dangerous threat
to India, but knew it needed to contain Napoleon.*

Nelson knew the French fleet was in the Eastern Mediterranean and
his search took him to Sardinia, Elba, Naples, Sicily, Alexandria and
back to Sicily. While he was returning to Egypt, his leading vessel
saw the French fleet at anchor in Aboukir Bay in Egypt, 15 miles (24
km) east of Alexandria and near the mouth of the Nile. The British

fleet arrived at around 5.30 pm on 1 August. Admiral Brueys, the French commander, had 13 ships of the line, including *L'Orient*, a three-decked man-of-war with 120 guns and the largest warship in the world. However, the French were wholly unprepared, there were no scouts and even when Brueys saw the British fleet he was certain they would not attack so late in the day. The French fleet was anchored at an angle across the bay in a defensive position, protected by a shore battery on a nearby island, but there were several weaknesses. The ships were at single anchor and could therefore swing with the wind and there were wide gaps between them and also between the ships and the shore. Many officers and men from the vessels were ashore at the time and there was an inadequate lookout.

Nelson's fleet was smaller but the wind was blowing into the bay so he decided to engage the enemy. His flagship, *Vanguard,* was in the middle of the line, with *Goliath*, commanded by Captain Thomas Foley, at the head. Seeing the gap between the ships and the edge of the shore, Foley took his ship across the bows of the French ship *Le Guerrier* and into the shallow waters behind. As Foley passed, he noted with satisfaction that the deck of the French ship was not prepared for war. Three warships followed the *Goliath* into the shallow waters. One ship, the *Culloden*, ran aground but the others successfully sailed through and lined up to open fire. Meanwhile, the rest of the British fleet led by Nelson was on the other side.

They opened fire at around 6.30 pm and the first eight ships in the French line suffered heavy casualties. Darkness fell within half an hour but the British came prepared with white lamps to be able to distinguish each other. They had the advantage but did not have it all their own way, as the *Bellerophon* was dismasted after being attacked by the French flagship *L'Orient*. Subsequently, the massive 120-gun *L'Orient* caught fire and blew up in a vast explosion causing much damage and illuminating the night, briefly stunning everyone. Just two French ships of the line and two frigates escaped, led by Villeneuve. It was a most decisive battle, although both sides suffered heavy casualties.

The Battle of the Nile. It was typical of Nelson's audacity that he mounted his attack in the early evening – although he did arm his ships with lamps in advance, so that they could recognize each other in the fading light.

Nelson sent off his despatches to the Admiralty in the *Leander* and ordered some of his ships to escort the six prizes to Gibraltar. He then travelled to Naples, unaware that his despatches did not reach London as the *Leander* had been captured. In the British government, meanwhile, there was much despondency. They knew that the French had landed in Egypt, and were now wholly alive to the risk to India, and there was much criticism of Lord Spencer, First Lord of the Admiralty, for choosing a young and inexperienced admiral to lead the Mediterranean fleet on such a vital mission. When the news of Nelson's success finally did arrive, declaring a complete victory at Aboukir, Lord Spencer fainted. Many of the elements of Nelson's leadership that were later in evidence at Trafalgar were used in the Battle of the Nile. As a consequence of this victory, Napoleon's army was cut off and the threat to India declined. Nelson was given a peerage, becoming Baron Nelson of the Nile, and honours and money were showered upon him – though not enough, he complained privately. He also became a national hero. Militarily, the battle also meant that the British now had control of the Mediterranean.

BATTLE OF COPENHAGEN

1801

In 1800, during the wars between Britain and France, Britain attempted to prevent other nations from trading with the French. In support of France, the Russians joined with Sweden, Prussia and Denmark–Norway to form the League of Armed Neutrality. The Baltic was crucial to Britain's war effort as the vital timber and naval stores were supplied from there and the pinch point was the narrow route between Sweden and Denmark. Denmark was doing well out of wartime shipping but there was a risk from the British perspective that it might become too closely allied with Russia.

Denmark put an embargo on British shipping in early 1801 and occupied Hamburg and Lübeck, thus closing the Elbe to British trade. The elderly Admiral Sir Hyde Parker was put in charge of a Baltic fleet and his second-in-command was Admiral Lord Nelson. Admiral Vincent, the First Lord of the Admiralty, had to push a reluctant Parker to set out. The Baltic fleet had two choices: either launch a pre-emptive strike against Copenhagen or sail past and attack the Russian fleet at Reval. They chose the former and, risking the Danish batteries in the narrow Sound, they passed through and anchored close to Copenhagen on 30 March.

Expecting some form of action, the Danish were well prepared and had heavily fortified their city. The naval dockyard was on an island with the narrow channel separating it from the city, making it potentially vulnerable to bombardment from the sea. Eighteen battleships and merchant vessels with heavy guns were moored in a line along the channel leading towards the city, in a similar fashion to the French when they had been moored at Aboukir Bay. A further seven ships guarded the entrance to the dockyard.

Urged on by Nelson, Hyde Parker sent him with 12 small ships of the line to attack while the larger ships and Hyde Parker remained at sea. Nelson had his flag on the *Elephant*, a small and manoeuvrable shallow draught 74-gun ship. Among his squadron was the 54-gun *Glatton*, commanded by Captain William Bligh. This vessel was an adapted East Indiaman equipped with 'carcasses', incendiary projectiles that were to be used effectively in the battle.

As the British squadron moved towards the city they rapidly encountered problems, as the Danes had removed all navigation buoys and sea marks in the shallow and narrow channels. Three ships, *Agamemnon*, *Bellona* and *Russell*, grounded on the Middle Ground, a large shoal at a distance from Copenhagen, but were still able to fire from their stationary position. The rest moved in to fight the Danish ships and the shore batteries. Unlike Aboukir Bay, the British could not get behind the Danish ships and initially the Danish guns were effective, particularly from the Trekroner Fort. Not only that but the Danes could easily reinforce their positions from the land. Gradually, however, the British gunnery prevailed. Each ship had been assigned a particular part of the Danish defences and by 1.30 pm they had effectively overcome the southern defences. Twelve Danish ships were out of action and the way was open for the bomb vessels to get within range. These heavily built vessels were specialists in shore bombardment, with mortars that fired explosive shells with a high trajectory.

Around this time, the anxious and cautious Parker, who was still 5 miles (8 km) away and could see little through the cloud of

The Battle of Copenhagen. Although seen as a good victory for the British, in that it removed Denmark from the Napoleonic Wars as a source of support to France, it was only a temporary end to hostilities. In 1807 the Royal Navy again successfully attacked Copenhagen, this time forcing a complete surrender of Denmark's forces.

gun smoke, ordered a general recall. A witness on board Nelson's ship later noted: 'Ld N. however never answered it ... the only signal which the hero kept flying was the very reverse viz Close Action.' The famous tale of Nelson putting his telescope to his blind eye is a myth, however. Nelson's captains followed his lead in ignoring the orders of their commander-in-chief. Rear Admiral Graves of the *Defiance* did hoist Parker's signal, but he ensured it was hidden behind a sail while continuing visibly to fly the signal for close action. As the balance of the battle began to favour the British, Nelson chose that moment to propose a ceasefire. It was a calculated if controversial action, to which the Danes agreed, enabling the wounded to be rescued. The position was something of a stalemate, with the bomb vessels still in place and Hyde Parker and his ships potentially available, but Nelson knew he still had to extract his ships and men from the narrow and shallow waters.

Nelson personally opened negotiations with the Crown Prince of Denmark, which took place over several days, and a truce was agreed on 8 April. There were about 254 British officers and seamen killed and 689 wounded in this battle and a slightly larger number of Danish casualties. On 4 May, Sir Hyde Parker was recalled to London and told to hand over to Nelson. Nelson sailed for Reval but there was no action, as the Russian Tsar had been murdered and Russian policy had changed, so an ailing Nelson, who was suffering from malaria, returned to England. Copenhagen had survived a British bombardment on this occasion and the way was open for the essential British trade with the Baltic. But in 1807, in a pre-emptive strike to avoid the Danish fleet being taken by Napoleon, the city of Copenhagen was totally devastated by British bombing and the Danish navy ships were captured and taken to England.

TRIPOLI (FIRST BARBARY WAR)

1801–1805

---

*The North African coast, particularly the areas of
Tunis, Tripoli, Algeria and Morocco, was notorious
in the eighteenth and early nineteenth century for
its acts of piracy. More than 150,000 Europeans
had been captured during the eighteenth century
and either enslaved or held to ransom. Positioned
by the narrow mouth of the Mediterranean, the
North Africans frequently attacked merchant vessels,
taking cargoes and hostages. Various countries
tried different methods to contain this problem and
many simply bought them off by paying a tribute,
essentially protection money. Britain had a treaty
with the North African states and also a powerful
navy, but, with American independence, it was open
season on American ships. In 1794, Congress passed
the Naval Act to re-establish the United States Navy
and the building of six naval frigates to defend
American interests, but these were limited in their
efforts to protect trade.*

By now, the US had signed treaties with each of the Barbary States to pay tributes and agree ransom for American prisoners, but Thomas Jefferson disagreed with this path and saw war as an alternative. He wrote that he 'was very unwilling we should acquiesce in the European humiliation of paying tribute to those lawless pirates.' In 1801, Jefferson became the third President of the United States and sent a naval squadron to the Mediterranean to protect commerce, and particularly targeted Tripoli. The Pasha of Tripoli had demanded even more money, repudiating a previous treaty with the United States, and declared war after failing to obtain any concessions. Four ships, the first US naval expedition overseas, were sent from Norfolk, Virginia, under Commodore Richard Dale to 'protect our commerce and chastise their insolence by sinking, burning, or destroying their ships and vessels where ever you shall find them'. The Dale mission was ineffective and the second mission was sent the following year under the command of Commodore Richard Morris, but it was also ineffective in restricting the actions of Tripoli.

By 1803, Jefferson was able to send further vessels under Commodore Edward Preble. The naval officer in charge of the USS *Enterprise* was Stephen Decatur. A hot-tempered young man from Philadelphia, the son of a merchant and privateer, Decatur joined the US Navy as a midshipman in 1798. Despite, or perhaps unhindered by, a reputation for fighting duels with fellow officers, he received his first command in 1803 and headed to the Mediterranean. Preble was successful in agreeing terms with Morocco and sent two ships, *Philadelphia* and *Vixen,* to blockade Tripoli. While chasing a Tripolitan vessel, the frigate *Philadelphia* under the command of Captain William Bainbridge ran aground on unmarked rocks. The ship was captured, together with its crew of 300, and taken into Tripoli. Pasha Yusef Kramanli gained a valuable and useful prize ship, recovered guns that had been thrown overboard and demanded a ransom of $3 million for the crew.

Preble, aware that the prestige of the nascent United States Navy was not high after two failed squadrons and now this capture, needed to take clear action. He could either try to invade Tripoli and retake the ship and prisoners or destroy the frigate. The odds were against a successful invasion, but Lieutenant Decatur had a proposal. His 14-gun schooner *Enterprise* had successfully captured a small Tripolitan vessel, *Mastico*. The plan was to take this vessel, which would look like any other local vessel, and recapture the *Philadelphia*. He was put in charge of the vessel, now named *Intrepid*, with a crew of 75 sailors and marines and provided with cover and support by the 16-gun brig *Siren* commanded by Lieutenant Charles Stewart. It was a highly risky and dangerous mission and only volunteers were taken. Commodore Preble insisted that the risk to the men was too great and that the *Philadelphia* was to be destroyed and no attempt taken to sail her out.

The two vessels left Syracuse, Sicily, on 2 February 1804, but once at the port of Tripoli storms prevented them from entering until 16 February, when the *Intrepid,* disguised as a Maltese vessel, managed to enter, leaving the *Siren* outside. As it entered the harbour, the *Intrepid* was guided by an Italian pilot, Salvatore Catalano. Once alongside the *Philadelphia*, 60 sailors and marines boarded their target and attacked the guards. They set fire to the vessel and made good their escape while *Philadelphia* became a fire ship within the harbour, deterring any pursuit. Although the *Philadelphia*'s crew remained hostage, the raid had not lost a single man. Nelson, who was in the Mediterranean with a blockade off Toulon, was impressed and declared it 'the most bold and daring act of the age.' American prestige was high and Decatur was praised by Preble for his intrepid actions and requested an immediate promotion for him. Decatur became the youngest captain appointed in the US Navy and received personal congratulations with his commission from the president.

Preble, meanwhile still had work to do and, assembling a large fleet at Syracuse with additional support from the King of Naples, he prepared a major attack on Tripoli. The attack in the summer of 1804 captured many prize ships and caused considerable destruction to the heavily armed harbour. However, it did not end the war and he returned to the United States in December having handed over to Commander Stephen Barron. Bainbridge and his crew were not released until the next year after what would become another famous action, this time by American marines. Lieutenant William Eaton led 400 mercenaries and seven marines across land from Alexandria to a victory at Derna, a hard passage of 600 miles (965 km). Derna, a port to the east of Tripoli, fell in the surprise attack and revealed the weakness of Tripoli. In exchange for $60,000, the Pasha released all American prisoners and agreed to a treaty ending the First Barbary War. This war was America's first conflict conducted on foreign soil and is proudly remembered in paintings, songs and the country's oldest military memorial, the Tripoli Monument, now in the US Naval Academy at Annapolis.

BATTLE OF PULO AURA

1804

British Admiral Peter Rainier was appointed to the command of the East Indies in 1794. It covered a vast territory of 30 million square miles (77.7 million sq km), at the heart of which was India. His key tasks were the protection of India from the French and the defence of the valuable trade with the Far East. However, he had a fleet of just 20 ships to cover this territory and his largest ship was a 64-gun warship. The large ships of the East India Company traded from England and the smaller country ships, as they were known, traded between India and the Far East. For safety, they often formed a convoy group and Admiral Rainier needed to know when a convoy sailed from China, and its route, to allow him to offer protection from his limited resources.

In January 1804, in Canton, the East India Company's China Fleet commanders prepared for their passage home. Their total cargo was worth £7 million, and the officers were only too aware of the impact of such a loss should it fall into the wrong hands. Technically, France and Britain were at peace, but rumours suggested that war was close. The fleet needed to decide when to sail to make the best of the weather on the long route home and whether to risk the Strait of Malacca, a narrow dangerous passage. An alternative was to go further east through Bali or Lombok. These routes, however, were not well charted and were again narrow, making it dangerous for a large and extremely valuable convoy. The other option was through the Sunda Strait between Sumatra and Java, which was more suitable for those heading directly to Europe. The decision was finally taken to go through the Malacca Strait. This was better for the country ships heading for India and the East India ships could also hope to get an escort for the convoy from Rainier for the Indian Ocean passage, which would pass the French-held island of Mauritius.

As they prepared, the *Ganges*, a fast sailing brig, arrived from Bengal with despatches and the news that France and Britain were again at war. The Dutch islands in the East Indies were now enemy territory since the occupation of the Netherlands by France. Commodore Dance, the 56-year-old commander of the China fleet, instructed all commanders to exercise their guns and small arms. The East India ships were large, the equivalent of a 64-gun warship, but were lightly armed. The *Earl Camden* and the *Warren Hastings* had ten 18-pound carronades on the upper deck and 26 similar guns on the main deck.

The fleet of 16 East India ships and 11 country ships left Canton, taking the fast-sailing *Ganges* with them as a scout. Also in the fleet was Lieutenant Fowler of the Royal Navy. His ship, the *Porpoise*, had been wrecked and he was now a passenger on the *Earl Camden* heading home. Aware of the dangers of the Malacca Strait the *Ganges* went ahead to Pulo Aura, an island just to the northeast of the entrance. On 16 February, with the fleet gathered closely together, the *Royal George* signalled the sighting of a suspicious group of four ships on the horizon. Dance ordered four of the East Indiamen, *Alfred*, *Royal George*, *Bombay Castle* and *Hope*, to go down and examine them and Lieutenant Fowler also went, transferring to the *Ganges*. They returned with the news that it was the French squadron under the command of Admiral Linois. This consisted of his 84-gun flagship,

Marengo, two heavy frigates, *Belle Poule* and *Sémilante*, a 26-gun corvette and an 18-gun Batavian brig, *William*. What happened next was a lesson in cool nerves and leadership worthy of Nelson.

Commodore Dance formed his large ships into a line of battle and sailed on, but the anticipated attack did not happen. By sunset Dance sent Lieutenant Fowler on the *Ganges* to position the country ships between the larger East Indiamen and the enemy. Fowler returned to the *Earl Camden* with volunteers from the country ships. The next morning, at 7 am, Dance hoisted his colours as a way of offering battle to the French, who were about 3 miles (5 km) to windward. The French also hoisted their colours. As the French attempted to cut off the rear, Dance made the signal to 'attack and bear down on him, and engage in succession'. The *Royal George* was in the lead, followed by the *Ganges* and *Earl Camden*. They sailed towards the French, holding their fire for as long as possible. The *Royal George* bore the brunt of the action and got as close to the enemy as it could. The *Ganges* and *Earl Camden* opened fire as soon as their guns could have effect, but before any other ship could get into action the French, thinking they were dealing with Royal Navy 64-gun third-rates, abandoned the action. Commodore Dance reported that they 'stood away to the eastward under all the sail they could set'. Seeing the French abandoning the fight, Dance made the signal for a general chase, and pursued them briefly until 4 pm. Concerned that they were now straying far from the Strait of Malacca, and with the French squadron now well in the east, the convoy regrouped to anchor for the night. In the morning they proceeded unimpeded through the Strait.

The *Royal George* had one man killed and another wounded and suffered minor damage to her hull and her sails. Few shots touched either the *Camden* or the *Ganges*, and, according to Dance, 'the fire of the enemy seemed to be ill directed, his shot either falling short or passing over us'. He singled out Captain Timins of the *Royal George* for his gallant action and praised all his brother commanders, whose ships were cleared and prepared for action. He found them and all the ships' companies 'unanimous in their determined resolutions to defend the valuable property entrusted to their charge to the last extremity'.

From Malacca, they were finally joined by a naval escort consisting of HMS *Albion* and HMS *Sceptre*, and the *Ganges* was sent with a letter to the Governor General of India, giving an account of the action to be forwarded to London. The convoy then proceeded to England via the Cape of Good Hope. On their arrival in London they were received as heroes. Lloyd's Patriotic Fund presented a ceremonial sword worth £100 to Dance and one valued at £50 was presented to each commander of the East India ships and also to Lieutenant Fowler. Commodore Dance was presented to the king and given a knighthood. He received an annual pension of £500 from the East India Company plus a lump sum of 200 guineas and a piece of plate worth another 200 guineas. Relief at the narrow escape of the very valuable convoy and admiration for the actions of the merchant fleet filled the newspapers.

BATTLE OF TRAFALGAR

1805

The period before the Battle of Trafalgar was as important as the battle itself. Successful battles need sufficient well-found, well-equipped ships and a good supply of well-trained and experienced seamen and officers. Additional factors in the successful outcome included the great team ethos among Nelson's 'Band of Brothers', the high regard all seamen had for their commander and the brilliance of his tactics.

The Peace of Amiens in 1802 was nothing more than an uneasy truce before hostilities recommenced in 1803, and in the meantime both sides took the opportunity to build up their fleets. The Royal Navy was heavily stretched. For a start, the protection of shipping in the North Sea was a high priority to ensure a regular flow of materials from the Baltic. Timber, flax for sails, pitch and tar were essential for new ships and the constant requirements for repair and maintenance. Then the blockades of Brest and Toulon took up resources and there was the Mediterranean fleet to maintain in order to support allies and check Napoleon. Plus there was Britain's involvement in the Peninsular War and the West and East Indies to guard.

In December 1804, the Spanish and the French agreed to combine fleets. However, the Royal Navy blockade meant that Villeneuve and his fleet were trapped in Toulon. Napoleon's plan to invade England depended on gaining control of the English Channel, so the intention was that the French fleets would break out of Brest, Rochefort and Toulon and combine with the Spanish navy to attack the British interests in the West Indies. The hope was that the Royal Navy would be forced to defend themselves and leave the English Channel open for an invasion. The Rochefort squadron did evade its blockade and in March 1805 Villeneuve's fleet also slipped out of its confines in Toulon. In April, Nelson received the intelligence that Villeneuve had passed out of the Mediterranean and was heading for the West Indies, together with the Spanish fleet out of Cádiz. He set out in pursuit while Cornwallis remained in the Channel, blockading Brest.

Villeneuve and Gravina, the Spanish admiral, arrived in Martinique, but after learning from a captured convoy that Nelson was now also in the West Indies they set sail back to Europe without having done any damage to British possessions on land or at sea. Nelson followed just two days behind. The Franco-Spanish fleet encountered a British squadron commanded by Admiral Calder near Cape Finisterre on 22 July and, in an abortive action, they lost two ships. Seeing his way barred to the Channel, Villeneuve headed for the safety of Cádiz. Nelson, still searching for Villeneuve, was keen to force a battle before the combined Spanish and French fleets stopped British shipping gaining access to the Mediterranean. However, once he was certain that Villeneuve had not re-entered the Mediterranean, Nelson briefly returned to England for his first shore leave for 27 months, leaving Collingwood to watch off Cádiz. By the end of September Nelson was once more with his fleet and briefing his officers.

Napoleon, who was by now on his fifth scheme for an invasion of England, continued to pressure Villeneuve to leave Cádiz to attack Nelson's fleet. Villeneuve was not anxious to meet Nelson, believing the British force was superior. In fact, the British fleet had now been reduced from 33 ships to 27, as six of Nelson's ships of the line had gone into Gibraltar for water and provisions. Nelson met his commanders to agree a plan of action. He wanted what he called a

Horatio Nelson. No one can say that Britain's greatest naval commander did not lead from the front. He lost the sight in his right eye in one battle and most of his right arm in another. His ability to inspire undying loyalty in his men was known in its day as 'the Nelson Touch', and his skills as a leader and motivator are still studied today.

'pell mell battle', and not a standard line of battle. Only too aware of the communication risks inherent in sea battles his orders included: 'In case signals can neither be seen or perfectly understood, no captain can do very wrong if he places his ship alongside that of an enemy.' Morale was high and Nelson's reputation was known throughout the fleet.

Jacob Richards, a landsman on *Euralyus*, wrote after the battle:

When the day broke the enemy's fleet was seen about 9 miles to leeward lying to and forming nine lines of battle in close order. Our brave Admiral made very few except telegraph signals having previously given to the Admiral's captains and commanders in the fleet such directions or instructions as were producing no doubt of the highest order and steadiness for battle.

Nelson had 27 ships, about 17,000 men and 2,148 guns, while Villeneuve had 33 ships, 30,000 men and 2,632 guns. Instead of a line of battle, Nelson organized three columns and he decided that he and his most senior commander, Collingwood, would lead their respective columns contrary to precedent. They also went into action with every sail they could muster, which meant that they closed on the enemy rather faster than expected. But even so the winds were not strong, which allowed plenty of time to prepare for battle and time for Nelson to compose his famous signal. This was raised at 11.40 am and read: 'England expects every man will do his duty.' Nelson had wanted to use the word 'confides', meaning 'trusts', but Lieutenant John Pascoe, the signal officer, explained that this required many more flags. It was a message that resonated throughout the fleet and variants of it were repeated in numerous letters home after the battle.

Nelson and Collingwood headed straight into the Franco-Spanish lines. As they came on at different speeds, to the enemy they looked like an untidy straggle. Villeneuve was on his flagship, *Bucentaure*, with the massive Spanish warship the *Santísima Trinidad* close by. Holding fire to conserve her ammunition and the energy of her crew, *Victory* suffered casualties. Iron discipline and strong nerves were needed, with one man beside Nelson killed outright. Twenty men were killed and 30 wounded before *Victory* opened fire at 12.35 pm.

Nelson's column cut vertically through the middle of the enemy fleet and Collingwood cut diagonally into the rear of the line. It was initially highly dangerous for the British fleet. Thomas Connell on board *Dreadnought* noted: 'We were exposed to breaking fire some time before we had it in our power to return the compliment.' But this unconventional attack caused considerable confusion to the Franco-Spanish fleet. While they had the advantage in the beginning, they were subject to a growing onslaught as more and more British ships piled into them. Firing began at midday and it came at a high cost. *Victory* was attacked by *Redoubtable* and at 1.15 pm Nelson, who was very visible in his full uniform and decorations, was hit in the shoulder by a shot fired from high in the enemy ship's rigging. The bullet shattered his spine and the surgeon, Beatty, knew there was little he could do. Villeneuve surrendered at 2.30 pm and Nelson died at 4.30 pm, having been told that he and his men had won a great victory.

An able seaman, James West of the *Britannia*, wrote to his parents:

I am sorry, and every British seaman too, for the noble hero Lord Nelson is no more. He died in the arms of victory, the glory of the world around him. They came out of Cadiz to take us, but the English hero defied them.

As they prepared to take the prizes and clear things up, a gale swept in causing considerably more damage to the battered and crippled vessels. Among all of this, Collingwood, now in command, needed to get urgent despatches back to England with news of the British victory, the death of Nelson, the casualty numbers, the prizes and the

The Battle of Trafalgar. This engagement took place off Cádiz, in southern Spain.

state of the fleets. By the end, 1,700 men in the British fleet had been killed or wounded and an estimated 6,000 French and Spanish men had been killed, with 20,000 taken prisoner. The frigate HMS *Pickle*, commanded by Lieutenant Lapenotière, was tasked with carrying the vital news with all speed to the Admiralty. What few ships were left of the Franco-Spanish fleet headed into Cádiz, while the British took their dead and wounded into Gibraltar.

In Britain the celebrations were muted, with news of Nelson's death being received as a personal loss by all levels of society. Eventually, the British fleet returned home. John Parr, a seaman, came into Plymouth with HMS *Hero* on 10 November: 'We came into harbour today with our prizes and met with a very kind reception from people on shore with loud Huzzas and bands of music playing "Rule Britannia".'

The French view was one of relative indifference. Napoleon had already given up on his invasion plans before Trafalgar, having to concentrate on land battles, and in December 1805 he won a decisive, much celebrated victory at Austerlitz. The greatest loser was Spain, whose fleet was totally destroyed. In 1806, Napoleon ordered a continental blockade, aiming to damage the British economically by preventing trade, but it had a bigger impact on the continental economies. Where Amsterdam had 80 sugar refineries in 1786, by 1813 this number had declined to just three. Portugal resisted the blockade, Spain rebelled, Sweden evaded it and Russia changed its mind. In 1809 Britain even imported grain from France.

As a result of the victory at Trafalgar, the British were undisputed rulers of the seas and remained so for the rest of the century. Every year in October the Royal Navy celebrates the victory at Trafalgar dinners, with the most senior officer present giving the famous toast to: 'The immortal memory of Nelson and those who fell with him.'

BATTLE OF THE AIX ROADS

1809

It is tempting to think that the Battle of Trafalgar, convincing as it was, totally annihilated the French fleet, but it was still a powerful force, although it had been dispersed between the various French ports of Brest, L'Orient and Rochefort. To avoid these ships combining and becoming a threat the British set up blockades.

Blockades worked well if the wind allowed, but bad weather forced the Royal Navy off their position and the French took the opportunity to slip out of Brest. The concern in London was that they might head for the West Indies where French Martinique was being besieged by the British. Instead, however, the ships from Brest headed down the coast and anchored with the Rochefort squadron in the Aix Roads and were now a force of 14 warships. This French concentration of warships caused concern in London and the commander-in-chief of the Channel Fleet, Admiral Lord Gambier, was instructed to destroy them with fireships. Contrary to the anxieties of his superiors at the Admiralty, Gambier, who was a cautious man, was unenthusiastic. He was a man of strong religious feelings and rejected the suggestion of the use of fireships.

Frustrated, the Admiralty sent for a young captain, Lord Cochrane, who was incidentally a Member of Parliament. Cochrane had earlier submitted plans to destroy the French fleet with the use of fireships and had been very successful in his young career as a fighting leader. Cochrane was shown the letters from Gambier and quickly recognized that the nation demanded action, but he also recognized that as a junior officer he would be in an invidious situation. If his plan succeeded the senior officer would get the credit but if it failed he alone would take the blame from both the Admiralty and the senior officer and with it the loss of his personal reputation. He also protested that his junior position meant that: 'Lord Gambier might consider it presumptuous on my part to undertake what he had not hesitated described as hazardous if not desperate.' But the Admiralty insisted and 12 fireships were prepared. Cochrane's plan also included a new weapon, the rockets invented by William Congreve.

Cochrane's fears were allayed when Gambier was only too happy to let Cochrane take charge of the fireships, although the other captains in the squadron who were senior to Cochrane were distinctly less impressed at being passed over. Cochrane took his ship *Imperieuse* and scouted the French fleet and fortifications. The fleet lay into lines protected by shallow waters and a floating boom.

On 11 April Cochrane at last had Gambier's approval for attack and decided that a night assault was the best option. In addition to the 12 fireships, Cochrane had three elderly transport ships in the squadron converted into explosive ships stuffed with logs, powder, shot and hand grenades. Then, together with three volunteers, he took the largest explosive vessel and led the ships towards the French. In the dark he sent his crew to the waiting boat and lit the fuse, and as they rowed back the ship blew up, shortly followed by the second explosive vessel as the fireships headed down through the boom. Just four reached the French and did little serious damage, but they caused panic as the French tried to evade them in the night and all but two of the French ships went aground.

In the morning, Cochrane signalled to Gambier suggesting an attack, but Gambier ignored it. Cochrane watched in frustration as the tide rose, which would enable the French ships to escape. Repeated signals to Gambier did nothing and Cochrane now made a bold and creative decision to force some action. He allowed his ship to drift stern first towards the enemy, gambling that if he was forced to engage the French ships the rest of the English fleet would have to come to his rescue. By 1.45 pm he was engaged with three French ships and Gambier had to take action by sending two warships and seven frigates. Three French ships surrendered and some of the smaller French ships were set alight by their crews; those that remained moved into the safety of the River Charente. The following morning Gambier recalled his fleet but, seeing the work had not been finished, Cochrane was determined to continue. Several ambiguous messages passed between the two men until Gambier told Cochrane to return to the fleet and then sent him with dispatches to England.

Cochrane was greeted as a hero and knighted, but rumours began to circulate about the unfinished business at Aix Roads, surfacing in the *Times* newspaper. When a House of Commons official vote of thanks to Gambier was proposed, Cochrane as an MP made it clear he would vote against it. Gambier decided to clear his name with a court-martial, which was heavily rigged in his favour. He was 'most honourably acquitted' and then, in the words of Professor Andrew Lambert, 'given the thanks of parliament for what was, under the most favourable interpretation, a gross error'. Cochrane was, in effect, accused of libel and it severely damaged his naval career. The whole affair was badly managed by a weak government.

THE WAR OF 1812

The United States declared war on Great Britain in June 1812. Anglo-American relations had been strained for some years and President Thomas Jefferson and his successor James Madison were supportive towards France. By 1812 there was a view in Washington that the French would be victorious, thus leaving Britain weakened. The Americans had an eye on Canada, whose population was just one tenth that of the United States. Canada supplied timber for shipbuilding, particularly for the Royal Navy, where their other timber supplies from the Baltic were threatened. Annexation of Canada would expand US territory while interrupting Britain's war effort.

It has been generally accepted that matters were exacerbated by the Royal Navy impressing American seamen to serve on their warships, although at the time it was standard practice in many nations to 'reclaim their subjects from foreign ships'. A particular challenge between Britain and the United States was how to define a British or American citizen: the first was by birth and the second by period of residence. There were no official US citizenship documents, although unofficial ones were issued by US consuls, but British officers were largely sceptical of any such paperwork. It has been estimated that about 6,500 US citizens were pressed in this way and about 3,800 were subsequently released, but it all added to the diplomatic pressure.

The British Army was preoccupied with the war against France, although the success of Trafalgar gave the Royal Navy considerable mastery of the seas. In response to the declaration of war, the British began with a naval blockade and sent five battleships from Halifax, Canada, to cruise off the coast. The US Navy had 11 frigates, three of which, *Constitution*, *President* and *United States*, were rated as 44-gun ships. USS *Constitution* was built in 1797 in Boston, one of six frigates of the new United States Navy. She had already seen action in two wars and was to be very successful in the War of 1812. The first major encounter was in August, when the 38-gun HMS *Guerriere* was heading back to Halifax for repairs and encountered USS *Constitution*. As they closed the distance between them, HMS *Guerriere* opened fire with broadsides, but the *Constitution*, despite the cannon balls hitting her side, held fire until the ship was closer. Her thick oak hull provided protection, which earned her the nickname 'Old Ironsides'. Captain Isaac Hull employed successful tactics in targeting the *Guerriere*'s masts and by 7 pm Captain James Dacres surrendered. Once the men left the ship, it was set on fire and sunk. It was a major coup for the US Navy and a shock to the British, but more was to come.

The 38-gun frigate HMS *Macedonian* had been taken by the 44-gun USS *United States* commanded by Stephen Decatur in October, when the larger ship brought down her opponent's masts and damaged the hull, causing the ship to surrender. Decatur was careful to preserve the ship and towed it into Newport, Rhode Island, where after repair it joined the US Navy as USS *Macedonian*. Decatur was later captured by the British in January 1815.

In December 1812, USS *Constitution* was just off Brazil under the command of Captain William Bainbridge and at 2 pm on 29 December it saw the 38-gun ship HMS *Java*. An opening salvo from *Java* damaged the *Constitution*, wounded Bainbridge and shattered the helm. Nevertheless, the *Constitution* closed in and delivered a broadside that destroyed the forward part of *Java*'s rigging. The two ships then became entangled and a final broadside from USS

Constitution finished the action. Captain Lambert and 60 British seamen were killed to just nine on USS *Constitution.*

Several other victorious single-ship actions followed. The sloop USS *Hornet* took the brig sloop HMS *Peacock* in February 1813 and the later Royal Navy court martial attributed the loss to 'want of skill in directing the fire, owing to an omission of the practice of exercising the crew in the use of guns for the last three years'. For the smaller British vessels in the West Indies there had been no serious fighting for many years. A weaker British ship against a US 44-gun vessel had two options: escape or fire from long range to disable masts and spars. The latter choice was not a British tradition, although in March 1814 the US frigate *Essex* was taken by HMS *Phoebe* doing exactly that.

HMS Shannon *overcomes the USS* Chesapeake. *The War of 1812 saw the fortunes of war ebb and flow between both sides, with no participant able to deliver a decisive knock-out blow. This ultimately led Britain and the US to seek a negotiated settlement to the conflict.*

In June 1813 HMS *Shannon* met USS *Chesapeake* off Boston. As a noted historian has pointed out, the warship is a complex system and one weakness in the system can bring about failure. This was the case with the *Chesapeake*. Captain James Lawrence in his confidence missed the fact that the ship had not been properly cleared for action. An early broadside brought the topsail yard down, causing the ship to turn into the wind, which enabled the British ship to rake fire across the deck, killing most of the officers. It was a British victory, but the US ships had shown their considerable skill in single-ship combat.

The War of 1812 showed the quality of the US Navy, sailors and ships. By 1814 the British had managed to establish a fairly tight blockade on the eastern seaboard of America, but both countries sought to escape from a war that was not achieving any objectives. A peace treaty was signed on 24 December 1814 in Belgium. At the end of the war the US Navy was seen to have performed extremely well and the single-ship actions had given it great popular success. USS *Constitution*, 'Old Ironsides' as she was known, became a national icon and remained in service until 1855.

BATTLE OF NAVARINO

1827

The last battle fought under sail was not between countries at war and, indeed, the battle itself was confused and probably began by accident. In 1827 there was considerable activity by various countries in the Mediterranean. The Russians were seeking to get access to the Mediterranean and the Greeks had risen against the Turks and were endeavouring to gain independence. While the British public was on the side of the Greeks, the government was doing its diplomatic best to mediate and was suspicious of Russian intentions. However, the Russians were opposed to Turkey and favoured Greece and there was also strong support for the Greeks in France, so a treaty was concluded in July between Britain, France and Russia. In September a verbal agreement was obtained from the Turkish commander for an armistice and all of the allies sent naval forces into Greek waters to monitor it. The Turks strengthened their position by an alliance with the Pasha of Syria and Egypt.

Vice Admiral Sir Edward Codrington of the Royal Navy was the most senior officer in rank and took command of the combined allied fleet. The Russian division was commanded by Rear Admiral de Heiden and the French by Rear Admiral Gauthier de Rigny. In total, the fleet comprised ten ships of the line, ten frigates and about 12 other vessels. The Turkish and Egyptian fleet was larger, but with fewer line of battle ships. The allies intended to enforce 'by cannon-shot if necessary, the armistice which was the object of the treaty; the object being to interpose the allied forces and to keep the peace by the speaking-trumpet if possible, but in case of necessity by force'.

Ibrahim Pasha, who was the commander of the Turkish fleet, had lined up his vessels in the Bay of Navarino and met Codrington and Rigny on 25 September. The allies offered mediation but Ibrahim Pasha said he could not leave the area until he knew the sultan's response to the offer of mediation. They then withdrew, leaving just two frigates to monitor the Turkish fleet.

Also in the area was a Greek naval division which was not part of Codrington's combined fleet. The Greek division was led by Lord Cochrane, a highly controversial British officer who had worked previously with the Chilean navy when that country was endeavouring to gain its independence. Ibrahim Pasha sent ships to demand that Cochrane and his Greek division withdraw but Codrington intercepted the Turks.

Considering the verbal treaty at an end, the Turkish forces on land were burning and plundering in Greece and attacking the town of Pylos. Concerned at the situation, Codrington decided to return to Navarino Bay to show force and try to contain the Turkish fleet. The weather was not suitable for a blockade so he decided to enter the bay. An eyewitness described the scene: 'Just as we reached the mouth of the port a Turkish boat came off to acquaint the Admiral that no ships were allowed to enter without permission from Ibrahim Pasha. The Admiral replied, that he came to give orders not to receive them; and that if they fired a single rifle shot at any of our ships, he would destroy the whole Turkish fleet.'

Led by Codrington, the allied ships sailed in and anchored close to the Turkish–Egyptian fleet. There was much tension and in the midst of this the *Dartmouth* sent a boat to a Turkish fire ship to request them to keep their distance. Thinking it had hostile intentions the Turks fired, killing the officer. The *Dartmouth* captain ordered covering fire to assist the returning boat's crew and at the sound of the gunfire firing broke out from all the other ships. It was highly confused, with indiscriminate firing everywhere and fire ships causing chaos on all sides. Not to be left out, the shore batteries also opened fire. The eyewitness account went on: 'The shots flew like showers of hail in all directions about the harbour, which was agitated like a cauldron of boiling water. The Turks fought dreadfully hard – much harder than we expected.'

The battle lasted about four hours and much of the Turkish fleet was destroyed and an estimated 4,000 Turks were killed or wounded, while the losses to the allies were 172 killed and 485 wounded. The anonymous witness reported on the aftermath:

A pasha had been with the Admiral, and asserted that the fire ships did not belong to their fleet, that they were of Modea, strangers to them. This I consider false – we knew they were fire ships before we entered the port; we also knew their positions, and the brigs of the squadron were ordered to secure them in the first instance … I forgot to mention, that all the Turkish ships which surrendered were destroyed by our ships the day after the battle. The Russians took some booty, and a few prisoners; but the English, and, it is believed, the French, did not bring away anything.

It was a wholly confused conflict, but the action ensured that Greece would survive as an independent country. Codrington was given awards by Russia and Greece and the Duke of Clarence, the First Lord of the Admiralty, insisted he was knighted. But the whole affair was

The Naval Battle of Navarino, by the French artist Ambroise Louis Garneray. Garneray was unusual in that he had been a sailor himself; and, for a time, a pirate. Not surprisingly, his work deals almost exclusively in nautical themes.

politically controversial and embarrassing to some in government, including the king. Codrington, much to his surprise, was returned to London and relieved of his command in June 1828, although he later resumed his naval career with other commands.

BATTLE OF HAMPTON ROADS

1862

The first battle between ironclad warships occurred during the American Civil War and it was to transform the nature of naval battles. Of the two ships involved in the epic battle, the Virginia *(ex* Merrimack*) of the Confederate Navy was a converted wooden steamship and the other, the* Monitor, *of the Union Navy, was purpose-built.*

Timber was still the predominant building material for naval ships but there had been much experimentation with the use of iron. The first large propeller-driven fully iron ship was the SS *Great Britain*, launched in 1843, but the world's navies were slow to adopt iron as a material for warships. France was the first country to build a wooden-hulled ironclad warship, *La Gloire*, in 1859, and the Royal Navy launched HMS *Warrior*, the first ship wholly of iron, and its sister ship, *Black Prince*, in 1860. These were all conventional-looking ships, but from the USA came the *Monitor*, a wholly different ironclad with a very different design.

Ironclads were considered by the USA in 1840 and in 1854 an investment was made in an experimental vessel called the *Stevens Battery*, a very advanced and complex design with multiple new ideas. However, with limited industrial resources available in the still-emerging nation it was never completed. But the Civil War brought great ingenuity to warship design at a time of need for both sides. The Confederate States had little in the way of a navy and five Union ships were blockading the Chesapeake. But then the Confederates raised a sunken wooden frigate, the USS *Merrimack*, which had been deliberately sunk and scuttled by the Union. The *Merrimack* was a steam screw frigate built in 1855 in Boston, which was nearly new but had unreliable engines. She was covered in thick iron plates, an iron ram was added to her bow and she was armed, but nothing could be done with her engines and they did not have the facilities to re-engine her. Her speed was slow but she was heavily armed. Captain Buchanan, an experienced naval officer in charge of the James River naval defences, took personal command and managed to pull together a crew of 350 out of local seamen and some men from the army.

It was a race against time as the Union was building a new and formidable ironclad warship in New York. Unlike the *Merrimack/Virginia*, the *Monitor* was designed as an ironclad and on completely new principles. Her designer, John Ericsson of Sweden, was a noted inventor. His vessel drew only 10.3 feet (3.1 m) of water and its deck was barely above the waterline. It also had a crew of only 50, compared to the *Virginia*'s more than 300. A news report described it as:

> ...*long, wide, and flat-bottomed vessel, with vertical sides and jointed ends, requiring but very shallow depth of water to float in, though heavily loaded with impregnable armour on her sides and with a bombproof deck. She is so low in the water to afford no target to the enemy, while everything and everybody is below the water line, with the exception of the men working the guns, who are protected by the shot-proof turret in which the guns are placed.*

It was a very strange shape, but as strong as its much larger rival and more manoeuvrable. The *Monitor* was able to work in half the depth of water required by the *Virginia* and had a large rotating turret with two 11-inch (28 cm) guns. It was built with great speed, as work began on 25 October 1861, and it was launched on 30 January 1862 and commissioned on 25 February. Lieutenant Commander Worden took command of the *Monitor* and left for the Chesapeake on 6 March. The ship was towed out of New York harbour by two wooden steamships. It was soon discovered, however, that she was not very seaworthy and in heavy weather was soon taking on water. However, she managed to make it into Chesapeake Bay late on 8 March.

That morning the *Virginia* had been towed out from its mooring. A press report described the sight: 'The sides, bow, and stern ... were covered with sloping iron plates extending two feet below the water-line, meeting above like the roof of a house. At her bows, on the water-line, were two sharp iron points resembling prows, six or seven feet apart.'

Accompanied by two Confederate steamers, *Yorktown* and *Jamestown*, she headed straight for the blockading Union ships, *Cumberland* and *Congress*, which were unprepared for the attack. Even as the *Virginia* closed within 100 yards (91 m) of them the Union ships could make no impact on her ironclad hull. With her iron battering ram on her prow the *Virginia* rammed the *Cumberland*, drew off and fired a broadside, then rammed again her again, sinking her. The *Congress*, which had been in a fight with the *Jamestown*, surrendered. Buchanan was highly successful despite the exceedingly unwieldy nature of his ship. Two ships were destroyed and a third damaged and there were 250 casualties, while just 21 of his own crew had been killed or wounded. Buchanan, who had been wounded in the leg, withdrew the *Virginia* close to the Confederate guns. At this stage the *Monitor* arrived in Hampton Roads just as it was getting dark.

In the morning at first light, *Virginia*, now under the command of Lieutenant Jones, headed across the bay to complete the destruction of the Union fleet, but the *Monitor* proved its worth, being easily

The Monitor and the Virginia engage. Looking more like early submarines than ships, these two vessels signalled the dawn of a new era of naval warfare.

manoeuvred and more able to work in shallow waters than the *Virginia*. The ensuing battle took most of the morning. Jones, finding that he could do little damage to the *Monitor*, targeted the *Minnesota* while at the same time trying to avoid the *Monitor*. Poor manoeuvrability caused the *Virginia* to go aground but a lucky shot temporarily disabled Captain Worden of the *Monitor*. He sustained eye injuries when a shell struck his pilothouse, which bought time for the *Virginia* to get away and fall back to the Confederate side.

Neither vessel was seriously damaged, but the battle was a strategic victory for the Union, which retained control of the north shore of Hampton Roads. The vessels never met again. By May Yorktown was captured, the city was abandoned by the Confederates and the *Virginia* was destroyed. Buchanan was promoted and was the most respected naval officer in the Confederate service, being recognized as an aggressive commander who was willing to challenge an enemy force regardless of its strength. He died in Maryland in 1870. John Worden had a long convalescence, during which he was visited by President Lincoln, who conveyed the thanks of Congress. Worden was promoted to commander in July 1862.

BATTLE OF CHERBOURG

1864

A significant naval battle of the American Civil War took place not in US waters but in the English Channel. It was not a battle of great fleets but a duel between two ships played out before an audience of curious sightseers and tourists.

While officially neutral during the Civil War, British shipbuilders built vessels for the Confederates. In August 1862, Cammell Laird shipyard at Birkenhead, near Liverpool, launched a three-masted ship with auxiliary steam engines which was apparently destined for the Turkish navy. The ship headed out for trials and was delivered to the Azores and her new owner, the Confederate Navy. Her commander, Captain Raphael Semmes, took on supplies of guns, ammunition and coal delivered by the *Aggripine* of London and officially commissioned his new ship as the CSS *Alabama*. Semmes and his crew then set off to target Union merchant shipping. The South did not have the naval resources of the North and so commerce raiding was one way of putting pressure on the Union by disrupting trade. Semmes had already been highly successful in his previous ship, the *Sumpter*, when he destroyed 17 Union merchantmen. Now, with the *Alabama*, he captured 26 merchant ships, while Union shipowners wisely began transferring their ships to foreign flags in order to protect them.

With his success in the Atlantic, Semmes moved to the South Atlantic and into the Indian Ocean. By the summer of 1864 he was back in Europe and on 11 June he was in Cherbourg requesting access for repairs. As a neutral state this caused concern for France and the Vice Admiral of the French naval dockyard, while allowing the ship to enter the port, was uncertain if the dockyard facilities could be used. He therefore sent the request for repairs to Paris. Land communications were now speedy thanks to the arrival of the telegraph in Europe and the USS *Kearsarge*, which was at Flushing, received a message from the United States consul in Paris regarding the whereabouts of the *Alabama*. The *Kearsarge* accordingly headed due south, arriving outside Cherbourg. Caught in the harbour, Semmes risked internment if he remained and, despite the state of his vessel, he decided to go out and fight. Knowing the likely outcome, he left all his papers on shore.

News spread about a possible conflict between the two ships. A 190-ton English steam yacht, *Deerhound*, was on the scene and, even more bizarrely, an excursion train carrying 1,200 Parisians was reported as coming to watch the spectacle from the shore. The *Alabama* came out at 10.30 am, steaming directly for the *Kearsarge*. However, the *Kearsarge* was fresh from port and well armed with two 100lb (45 kg) guns. Furthermore, John Winslow, the captain, once a friend of Semmes', had protected the vulnerable part of his wooden vessel with anchor chains and hidden this protection with planking. The *Alabama*'s advantage of speed was compromised due to her state of repair, but she opened fire first and aimed at the rigging of her opponent. Each ship endeavoured to get behind the stern of the other, which would have enabled them to attack from the least protected perspective, and they circled each other, watched by the spectators. In the manoeuvring both vessels made seven complete circles at distances of between a quarter and a half mile (0.4–0.8 km). The *Kearsarge* had the advantage of a better-trained crew and her shots were more accurate. After an hour a shot from the *Kearsarge* damaged the *Alabama*'s engines and Semmes realized this was the end. In an effort to save as many of his crew as possible he surrendered, but they only had one serviceable boat.

Watching all of this were the spectators on board the private yacht, *Deerhound*, which had on board John Lancaster, a Lancashire coal mine owner, and his wife plus their daughter, two sons and a niece. By 12.30 pm the Confederate vessel was sinking. The *Deerhound* immediately made towards her and when she passed the *Kearsarge* Captain Winslow shouted: 'For God's sake do what you can to save them.' When the *Deerhound* was still at a distance of two hundred yards (183 m) the *Alabama* sank, and the *Deerhound* then lowered her boats and succeeded in saving 39 men, including the captain and 13 officers. Two boats from the *Kearsarge* picked up around 70 of the other survivors. The losses sustained by the *Alabama* were two men drowned and six men killed and one man was killed on the *Kearsarge*. The *Kearsarge* took its rescued survivors to Cherbourg while the *Deerhound* headed for the nearest British port, Southampton.

Semmes and his men thanked Lancaster for his help. 'Gentlemen,' Lancaster replied, 'you have no need to give me any special thanks. I should have done exactly the same for the other people if they had needed it.' The *Deerhound*'s intervention was roundly criticized by anonymous letter writers and enraged Captain Winslow, who was firmly of the opinion that the *Deerhound* should have handed over Semmes and his men to him as prisoners. The American ambassador was sent a despatch directing him to 'demand of the British government the restoration of Semmes and his fellow pirates' and further declared that the carrying of them by the *Deerhound* to Southampton was a hostile act towards the United States. But Lancaster defended his principles and the British government refused to comply. In France the same attitude was taken regarding the men who had been landed on French soil.

Semmes was lionized in England, and after touring Europe for several months he returned to the Confederacy to a hero's welcome and was made a rear admiral. John Winslow was criticized for losing the prisoners and even accused of treachery, but his destruction of the *Alabama* made him a hero. He was promoted to commodore and the New York Chamber of Commerce presented him with a gift of $25,000 for eliminating such a notorious commerce raider.

BATTLE OF MANILA BAY

1898

At Manila Bay, the United States Navy had the most complete victory in their history when they destroyed the Spanish fleet in the Pacific without losing one man or one vessel. In the last decade of the nineteenth century, countries were vying for control of Southeast Asian ports. The Russians had secured Port Arthur in China, much to the displeasure of the British, while, in the Philippines, the local populace was attempting to throw off Spanish rule. Nearer home, there was tension between Spain and the United States over Cuba, where there were also revolts against Spanish rule, and the popular opinion in the United States was very anti-Spain. The US Navy was emerging as a significant naval power and the Maine *was one of its newest battleships. The ship was on a diplomatic mission to Havana in February 1898 to provide support should the riots attack American property when an explosion ripped through the ship, killing 250 officers and men. This incident was a key factor in President McKinley's decision to declare war on Spain.*

Attention turned to Southeast Asia and the Spanish-controlled Philippines. The right man was needed to command the Asiatic station for the US. The Assistant Secretary of State of the Navy, the energetic Theodore Roosevelt, knew whom he wanted in the post, and it was not Commodore Howell, whom he described as '... an honorable man, and a man of great inventive capacity, but I have rarely met one who strikes me as less fit for a responsible position. He is irresolute; and he is extremely afraid of responsibility.'

Roosevelt wanted Commodore George Dewey in the role. Dewey had a long naval career and most recently had been based in Washington as President of the Board of Inspection and Survey, presiding over the building of five American battleships. After some careful manoeuvring, Roosevelt got his way, and Dewey was given the post as commander-in-chief.

In their conflict with Spain, the United States had been planning an attack on the Philippines, but such an operation conducted at long range needed plenty of advance preparation. The United States consul in Manila had provided much useful local information until he was told to leave by the Spanish government. War was declared between the United States and Spain and this information was conveyed to Dewey on 23 April. Dewey was already on station just off Hong Kong and his official orders were: 'Proceed at once to Philippine islands. Commence operations particularly against Spanish fleet. You must capture vessels or destroy. Use utmost endeavour.'

The Asiatic Squadron had the ironclad cruisers *Olympia, Boston* and *Raleigh*. Dewey had additional ships from San Francisco, the *Concord* and the *Baltimore,* plus a revenue cutter *McCulloch*. He also purchased a collier, *Nanshan,* and a British supply ship, *Zafiro,* and took them into his fleet. The fleet was in Mirs Bay, where he was joined by Oscar Williams, the consul, on 27 April, and the squadron set off for Manila.

Rear Admiral Patricio Montojo was the commander-in-chief of the Spanish Navy in the Philippines. His fleet consisted of seven

The Battle of Manila Bay. This was a one-sided affair that established the US as a growing imperial power, especially in Southeast Asia.

unarmoured ships and the largest vessel was wooden. Additionally, they were in poor condition, not having been maintained or repaired well. The coastal defences were also weak, so Admiral Montojo took the decision to meet the opposition in Manila Bay. Dewey's fleet met them there on 1 May, having passed the coastal batteries. Montojo had stationed his ships in the shallow bay, knowing he was out-gunned and with the hope that his men might more easily be rescued in what he knew was a hopeless fight.

In the early morning, Dewey's fleet headed towards Manila Bay, and at daybreak they saw the shipping in Manila. Shore batteries opened up but the shells fell short. A small torpedo boat came out and headed for them but was driven back and eventually was damaged and had to beach. The USS *Olympia* led the column towards the Spanish ships and they hit the Spanish flagship *Reina Cristina* and the others. At 7.35 am, Dewey was told they were low on ammunition and so he ordered a move back out into the bay and then coolly sent all the men to breakfast. When he was informed that they did, in fact, have plenty of ammunition, Dewey ordered a second assault on the Spanish ships. These were now largely on fire and abandoned, and only one, the *Don Antonio de Ulloa,* and some shore batteries returned fire. Accordingly, Dewey attacked and entirely destroyed the Spanish fleet with limited damage to his ships.

Making contact with the Spanish Governor of Manila via an intermediary, who was the master of a British merchant vessel, Dewey offered to withhold bombardment of the city in return for the shore batteries ceasing to fire. But the governor refused a request to allow the Americans to use the telegraph, so Dewey severed the line. As a result, it was a week before Dewey's report could be sent via Hong Kong to Washington. Meanwhile, Dewey had to blockade Manila while waiting for troops with which Manila could be seized and held.

In June 1898, the United States invaded Cuba, and the capital Santiago surrendered. Manila was eventually taken in August without bloodshed by an American force of 10,000 men. In the ensuing peace, both the Philippines and Cuba were ceded to the United States. The Americans proclaimed Dewey a national hero for his complete victory over the Spanish fleet.

BATTLE OF TSUSHIMA

1905

In February 1904 a group of Russian warships anchored outside Port Arthur on the Chinese mainland were unexpectedly attacked by Japanese torpedo boats. Three hours later Japan formally declared war on Russia and followed up its surprise attack by blockading the port and landing troops and guns, thus sealing off the remaining Russian ships in the port. Russia needed to get reinforcements to the area fast, but geography was a severe limitation.

Russia, with its great landmass, was ever eager to gain access to the sea. It had access through the Baltic, but in the Black Sea movements through the Dardanelles into the Mediterranean were restricted. In the Far East, Russia's port of Vladivostok was inaccessible in winter so it had signed a lease with China in 1898 to establish a base at Port Arthur, about 250 miles (400 km) to the east of Beijing. Meanwhile, Japan had overrun the Korean peninsula, where Russia had mining and logging interests.

The response to the Port Arthur attack was to send the Baltic fleet. Russia had an ageing fleet but it was building new battleships to counter the Japanese threat. By September 1904 it had four new battleships. In command was 56-year-old Admiral Rojestvensky, whose experience had been largely staff-based with limited time at sea.

The fleet left the Baltic on 14 October in his flagship, the *Souvaroff*, one of the new battleships of 13,500 tons. The squadron comprised 45 ships, including transport ships and a hospital ship. The plan was to forge the squadron and train the crew on the long passage to Vladivostok, via the Cape of Good Hope. The distance was nearly 18,000 miles (28,968 km), with no friendly Russian bases and there were strict rules regarding the very limited support that could be given to opposing sides by neutral countries.

The squadron stopped at Tangiers and was able to coal. The fleet then divided into two, sending one small group via the Suez Canal under Rear Admiral Folkersam. The two parts of the fleet were to meet again at Madagascar and the world watched as the Russians headed off to the Cape. Folkersam arrived at the appointed rendezvous first, having taken a shorter route, and by mid January 1905 had been joined by the rest of the fleet. Rojestvensky's ships had experienced frequent mechanical breakdowns on the way and had encountered difficulties in getting coal along the route. Folkersam's ships also needed repairs if they were going to take on the well-trained and well-equipped Japanese navy, which was battle-ready and waiting, having just fully taken Port Arthur and destroyed the Russian ships in the harbour.

Rojestvensky was told that more ships were coming from St Petersburg, commanded by Rear Admiral Nebogatoff, but these ships were old and not fit for modern warfare. Viewing them as a potential liability rather than a help, and reluctant to be burdened with them, Rojestvensky left Madagascar as quickly as possible and had crossed the Indian Ocean and sailed through the Malacca Strait by April. The coal-fuelled squadron made the long uninterrupted passage of 4,500 miles (7,242 km) from Madagascar and through the Strait to anchor at Cam Ranh, in modern-day Vietnam, but here Rojestvensky was given strict orders to await Nebogatoff and his ageing fleet.

After a two-week delay the combined fleet was off Shanghai and contemplating the final passage. To get to Vladivostok there were several choices of route, with the most straightforward being through the Straits of Korea, but it was also the most exposed. A meeting with the Japanese was inevitable. The weather seemed to be on the side of the Russian fleet, with patchy fog, and in columns they headed for the passage between Tsushima Island and the Japanese mainland. However, they were seen by a Japanese scouting cruiser which was able to send a signal to Admiral Tōgō, using the wireless technology, that read: 'Enemy fleet in sight in square 203 apparently making for the eastern channel.'

Admiral Tōgō, in his flagship *Mikasa*, had six battleships and six armoured cruisers and a further division of cruisers and destroyers at his disposal. Tōgō was aged 58 and spoke excellent English, having spent seven years in Britain, where he trained as a cadet. He positioned his ships in the centre of the Straits and waited. The Russian ships appeared at 1.45 pm on 27 May 1905, and both commanders hoisted signals to their respective fleets.

Tōgō turned his heavy ships at right angles to the approaching Russians and sent other vessels to attack the rear. Rojestvensky opened fire at 9,000 yards (8.2 km), but Tōgō held until the gap was 6,500 yards (6 km) and attacked the flagships of the two divisions. Within 20 minutes one of those, the *Oslyabya*, was badly hit and began to sink. A few minutes later the other flagship, *Souvaroff*, was disabled. The Japanese big guns and effective aiming had prevailed after just 30 minutes. The next ship in the firing line was the *Imperatur Alexander III* and she capsized and sank with just four survivors.

By 5 pm, the remaining Russian ships were still being attacked from the east and the south. Admiral Rojestvensky, who was wounded, handed over to Admiral Nebogatoff and ordered him to proceed to Vladivostok. Nebogatoff attempted to force his way north with a few ships, including two of the most modern vessels, the *Borodino* and the *Orel*. As Tōgō pursued them the *Borodino* was hit and blew up. The scattered Russian fleet disappeared into the dark and Tōgō ordered his torpedo boats to go into operation. The battle was now spread across

150 miles (241 km) and in the morning what was left of the Russian fleet was surrounded by the Japanese. Nebogatoff surrendered and in the end just three of Rojestvensky's fleet, two destroyers and a light cruiser, actually arrived at Vladivostok.

The Japanese had lost around 600 men, with damage to one armoured cruiser and two light cruisers and half a dozen destroyers needed repairs. On the other hand, the Russian fleet had been wiped out and around 6,000 Russians had perished. Rojestvensky was captured by the Japanese and was visited by a courteous Admiral Tōgō while in hospital.

The Times newspaper observed that 'It establishes past all dispute the supremacy of Japan over her adversary at sea', and others commented on Russia's costly and disastrous adventure: 'The moral to be drawn from the battle of the Sea of Japan is that it is necessary to have big ships, possessing great stability, that the crews must undergo a long course of gunnery practice in all weathers, and that marksmen are as valuable as a good admiral.'

Three weeks later President Roosevelt enabled a peace treaty between the two nations, which required the evacuation of Port Arthur and Manchuria by the Russians. In Russia, the disastrous naval expedition led to the 1905 Revolution. Internationally, Admiral Tōgō was the great hero and was much admired, receiving an OBE from King Edward VII in 1906. Tōgō himself spoke of comparisons with Admiral Nelson.

BATTLE OF THE FALKLAND ISLANDS

1914

In November 1914, Vice Admiral Maximilian von Spee was leading his East Asiatic Squadron from the Western Pacific to the coast of Chile. The squadron comprised two large armoured cruisers, Scharnhorst *and* Gneisenau, *plus the light cruiser* Leipzig *and two fast scout cruisers,* Nürnberg *and* Dresden. *Off the port of Coronel in Chile, they met a British squadron under the command of Rear Admiral Sir Christopher Cradock, who had two large armoured cruisers,* Good Hope *and* Monmouth, *a light cruiser,* Glasgow, *and an auxiliary vessel,* Otranto, *which was a converted ocean liner. The Germans, with their heavy armament and well-trained gun crews, sank both of the British large cruisers with the loss of those on board and the other two vessels managed to escape.*

The defeat was a shock to Britain, who had expected so much of their navy. Admiral Sir John Fisher had been appointed as First Sea Lord 48 hours before and his reaction to the news was swift. He sent two battlecruisers, *Invincible* and *Inflexible*, to the South Atlantic under the command of Vice Admiral Doveton Sturdee. Sturdee then met up with Rear Admiral Stoddart's squadron of three armoured cruisers, *Carnarvon*, *Cornwall* and *Kent*, plus two light cruisers, *Bristol* and *Glasgow*. The latter, commanded by Captain Luce, had survived the Battle of Coronel. Combining just off the coast of Brazil they then moved south towards the Falklands. Although they were attempting to conserve fuel they were urged on by Luce, who felt speed was essential. They reached Port Stanley on 7 December.

Meanwhile, the Germans had remained in Chile during November and were well aware of the risk posed by the Royal Navy. Even so, they viewed the opportunity of inflicting further damage on the British shipping concentrated in the South Atlantic as too good to miss. They headed out on 26 November into bad weather and eventually rounded Cape Horn on 1 December. The next day they captured a British merchant vessel which was loaded with coal and took the opportunity to refuel their ships, which took several days. During that time Spee, his captains and his crews enjoyed some onshore leisure. On 5 December, Spee called a meeting to discuss their plans, which were to head for the Falkland Islands, destroy the wireless station there and use the islands' coal supplies to refuel in order to get home.

On the morning of 8 December the *Canopus*, an old battleship, was stationed outside the harbour and some of her lighter guns were mounted in batteries ashore with an observation point. The two British battlecruisers *Invincible* and *Inflexible* were inside the harbour, coaling. Spee sent the *Gneisenau* ahead with *Nürnberg* to reconnoitre and their crews saw just three cruisers and one light cruiser. As they headed towards the port they were sighted by the observation point at 7.50 am. When the German ships drew near, *Canopus* opened fire with both of her 12-inch (300 mm) guns and the *Gneisenau* turned away and steered to the southeast. Rejoining Spee, the ships' crews reported seeing tripod masts in the harbour, denoting battleships. Although he believed they were mistaken, Spee ordered his ships to head southeast at top speed. After frantic work by the British to ready their ships for sea, *Invincible* and *Inflexible* steamed out of port.

It was a clear day with blue skies, a calm sea and excellent visibility and Sturdee signalled 'General chase' as the German warships headed rapidly away. As the British closed in, Spee signalled his fleet to separate and *Dresden*, *Nürnberg* and *Leipzig* then detached themselves. Sturdee sent *Glasgow*, *Kent* and *Cornwall* in pursuit, leaving him with the two heavier German battleships. *Invincible* targeted *Gneisenau* and *Inflexible* opened up on *Scharnhorst*.

Sturdee's ships had the more powerful, longer-range guns and greater speed, while Spee's flagship, the *Scharnhorst*, had the German navy's gold medal for gunnery. The British ships opened fire at just after 1 pm and the battle was fought over several hours, often in thick gun smoke. Three hours later, despite impressive gunnery, the *Scharnhorst* sank with all on board and, resisting to the end, the *Gneisenau* sank around an hour later. A contemporary news report wrote:

> *The Germans fought it out with characteristic courage to the very end, the* Scharnhorst *going down by the stern, with the admiral's flag flying from the main yard. The* Gneisenau *went under a little later; and after a spirited action the* Glasgow, *which was in the Chilean fight, sunk the* Leipzig. *Subsequently the* Nurnberg *was overtaken and sent to the bottom. The* Dresden *escaped and is still at large.*

German casualties were very heavy, including the entire crew of the *Scharnhorst*. In total 1,871 men were lost and 215 were rescued, although some later succumbed to shock from the freezing waters, while the British casualties were comparatively slight; six men were killed and several wounded. In the clear weather and calm seas the Germans were 'outnumbered, outgunned and outpaced' by their opponents. It was a significant victory that had destroyed a serious threat to merchant shipping and the defeat of Coronel was avenged. The British Admiralty ordered further battlecruisers combining high speed and heavy gun power.

BATTLE OF JUTLAND

1916

*Admiral Jellicoe had little idea of the location of
the German battle fleet in 1916. While he had a
powerful navy under his command with all the
latest technology, he was also very aware that
there were other weapons, such as the U-boat, that
could be deployed by the Germans. Jellicoe's fleet
had its main base in the Orkneys at Scapa Flow,
and despite several occasions when they left their
moorings to search for the enemy they did not meet
them in 1914 or in 1915 as the German fleet rarely
left its base, preferring to avoid a full fleet action
and instead maintain a war of attrition by attacking
individual ships or groups of ships.*

Vice Admiral Scheer was appointed the commander-in-chief of the
High Seas Fleet in 1916 and an early decisive action was the
bombardment of Lowestoft and Great Yarmouth in April by German
battlecruisers. This unexpected attack on the British mainland put
great political pressure on the Royal Navy to take action.

On 30 May intelligence came that the German High Seas Fleet was
preparing to put to sea. That evening Jellicoe led his ships out of Scapa
Flow and from Rosyth came the battlecruiser fleet commanded by Vice
Admiral Beatty in his flagship *Lion*, which consisted of 50 warships.

At 2.40 pm, Beatty encountered the German scouting group led by Rear Admiral Hipper and at around 4.00 pm both sides opened fire. But before the battleships led by Evan-Thomas could come to Beatty's support the German battlecruiser *Von der Tann* hit the *Indefatigable*, which blew up when shells caused catastrophic explosions in incorrectly stowed ammunition. Just two of the 900 men on board were saved. The next casualty half an hour later was the powerful battlecruiser *Queen Mary*, which sank after an explosion in one of her main magazines. Of her crew of 1,200 men just 20 were saved. Meanwhile, Admiral Scheer was heading northwards with his High Seas Fleet to support Hipper. Beatty's task was to draw them north into the path of the main British battle fleet. Jellicoe's fleet was cruising at 20 knots, its maximum speed, and was in six columns of four ships. He sent Rear Admiral Hood ahead with his three battlecruisers, which could travel at a faster speed, and they came to the support of Beatty.

As Jellicoe saw the battleground and the heavy gun smoke covering much of it he deployed his 24 battleships into a single line. Now the smaller squadrons needed to remove themselves to allow the big battleships to do their work. Due to the thick gun smoke accurate gunnery was difficult. HMS *Defence* was hit repeatedly and blew up with all hands. The third major British casualty was Hood's flagship *Invincible*, which exploded with just six men out of the crew of 1,000 surviving. Admiral Scheer ordered an emergency turn away and, in a display of highly effective seamanship, the German fleet simply left the battlefield. But half an hour later he turned again into the British line and ordered his torpedo boats into action. Jellicoe turned his fleet away, evading the torpedo threat but allowing Admiral Scheer to escape.

Beatty had one more opportunity to tackle the German navy and the *Pommern* was blown up by a torpedo from HMS *Onslaught*, but by daylight there was little to see except wreckage and bodies. The German navy claimed victory as the British had lost three battlecruisers, three armoured cruisers and nine destroyers, while the German losses

The Battle of Jutland was inconclusive, with both sides claiming victory. Even today there is no consensus, though it is agreed that both Britain and Germany achieved some of their strategic aims.

were just one old battleship and one battlecruiser, four light cruisers and five destroyers. But they knew they had been very lucky. The remaining British fleet was soon back in service and Jellicoe could report to the Admiralty that he still had 24 dreadnoughts ready for sea, while the German damage was much greater. Scheer could only muster ten, so Germany focused on submarine warfare.

The overall result was much less decisive than Britain hoped, although in the long term it did deter the German Grand Fleet. But it was not the great victory anticipated and there were plenty of recriminations, with cautious Jellicoe being unfavourably compared to the rather more dashing and photogenic Beatty.

Jellicoe wrote on 4 June 1916 to Arthur Pollen, a journalist and naval commentator:

What bad luck we had!! Simply and solely a question of low visibility. You could see only 5 to 6 miles when I got into action and it was a most confusing situation. One could see flashes of guns in all directions, shell bursting and falling, ships blowing up, and a very occasional glimpse of the enemy. His battle fleet turned away each time we got at him and disappeared in mist. We slated them hard for the short time we got at them. I never saw Iron Duke *do better. Her opening salvo short. Up 800 yards. Over. Down 400. Hit a Koenig with three salvos in succession. Then she disappeared in the mist. We had another go at one later and at light cruisers, also had two torpedo boat attacks to counter. It is most difficult to get enemy losses but they were certainly heavy.*

Our battlecruisers showed up their terribly weak point of want of protection as compared with the German. The public should know how poorly they compare in this respect. Perhaps you will tell them! It is of course all public information but the public only looks at guns and never at armour. In justice to our ships I think the point should be brought out very clearly ...

Lessons were learnt from the ruins of Jutland but there was not to be another great encounter in World War I. From the high point after the Battle of the Falklands, the Battle of Jutland destroyed the reputation of the battlecruiser. The Royal Navy's resources were stretched and faith in the Admiralty was at its lowest point, while the vital supply lines across the Atlantic were now vulnerable to German submarines.

BATTLE OF THE
RIVER PLATE

1939

*As the noted naval historian Professor Eric Grove
has written, 'That the Royal Navy owed its success
in 1939 not to the employment of superior firepower
but to tactical skill and aggressive determination
showed how much times had changed from the
assured material supremacy of earlier years.'*

The German navy had been limited by the Treaty of Versailles to a maximum size of 10,000 tons. In the 1930s three warships were built and became known as 'pocket battleships'. Designed as long-range commerce raiders, they had six 11-inch (280 mm) guns and comparatively light armour protection, relying on speed to avoid major confrontations.

Two of these were deployed in the Atlantic. The *Deutschland* was sent into the North Atlantic and the *Admiral Graf Spee* to the South Atlantic. Admiral Eric Raeder, the commander-in-chief of the German Navy, instructed his commanding officers that they should not engage with warships but instead should concentrate on individual merchant vessels and avoid the well-protected convoys.

The North Atlantic convoys meant that the *Deutschland* had little opportunity, but in the south almost all ships sailed free of convoys. *Graf Spee*'s captain, Hans Langsdorff, was adept at commerce raiding and by the end of October had succeeded in causing disruption to Allied trade by sinking or capturing five merchant ships around the Cape of Good Hope.

When an unidentified German ship began raiding British vessels, the Allies formed seven groups to hunt it down. One of these groups, known as Force G, was led by Commodore Henry Harwood, commander of the Royal Navy's South American Division, who had four cruisers deployed on the southeast coast of South America. Tracking the raider down was an almost impossible task in a vast ocean. But fortune played its part.

At the end of November *Graf Spee*'s engines needed serious attention and, aware that at some stage he would have to return to Germany, Langsdorff sought a major victory with the Royal Navy to make his mark. On 2 December, he boarded and sank a cargo liner, the *Doric Star*, and on the following day he sank the *Tairoa*. On 6 December, Langsdorff refuelled from his auxiliary vessel, *Altmark*, and then transferred most of his prisoners to that ship, with the exception of any officers or radio operators. Langsdorff's habit was to take a captured ship's crew prisoner before he sank it.

The *Streonshalh*, *Graf Spee*'s final victim, encountered Langsdorff's ship on 7 December. Before taking the crew prisoner and sinking her as usual, *Graf Spee*'s crew found confidential information suggesting that the Plate estuary would be a good place to target merchant shipping.

Langsdorff was particularly attracted by the description of a small convoy due to leave Montevideo on 10 December. Reckoning that such a small convoy might just have a very light naval escort, Langsdorff decided this would be his big prize. Harwood, meanwhile, had also decided to make for the Plate, guessing that this area would be a magnet for Langsdorff. It was a fortunate guess, as signals from Langsdorff's victims, the *Doric Star* and the *Tairoa*, had pinpointed them as being off the African coast. Unknown to Harwood at the time was another piece of fortune in that the *Graf Spee* had no aerial reconnaissance support due to engine problems with its Arado seaplane.

On 13 December, the crew of the *Graf Spee* sighted three smaller warships. Despite being reminded by his navigating officer of instructions not to engage with enemy warships, Langsdorff decided these were ideal targets and at 6 am he headed southwest towards them.

What Langsdorff found was Henry Harwood in his light cruiser *Ajax*, armed with eight 6-in (150 mm) guns, and its sister ship *Achilles* and the 8,000-ton heavy cruiser *Exeter*, with six 8-inch (200 mm) guns. This was not the light prey the Germans had assumed.

Additionally, they were speedier than the *Graf Spee*, whose worn-out engines limited her speed. Captain Bell of the *Exeter* then put Harwood's plans into action. Harwood had thought carefully about his intended meeting with the pocket battleship and had decided that two divisions would attack from different directions. So the *Exeter* went west as Harwood continued northeast. As the larger threat, the *Exeter* drew accurate German fire and was soon hit, with one shell going through the ship and the other hitting the bridge and killing all except 'the captain and two others'.

Harwood's plan was working, while the *Exeter* was still able to fire. The Germans now had to attend to the *Ajax* and the *Achilles*, which were attacking from the other side. The *Exeter* then managed to fire her torpedoes. Langsdorff and his officers were only too aware of the serious threat presented by torpedoes, so they turned towards the northwest just half an hour into the engagement.

In the exchange of fire that followed 36 of *Graf Spee*'s crew were killed whereas 61 sailors died aboard *Exeter*. *Ajax* and *Achilles* got off lightly, with seven killed on *Ajax* and four on *Achilles*. But *Graf Spee* had been badly damaged and was now unseaworthy. At 7.40 am Langsdorff decided to make for Montevideo in Uruguay, on the north side of the River Plate, in order to attempt repairs. *Graf Spee* dropped anchor in Montevideo in the early hours of 14 December. However, under the Hague Convention a belligerent warship could only remain in a neutral port for 24 hours, added to which Uruguay was on the side of the Allies.

The Admiral Graf Spee sinks. Her commander, Hans Langsdorff, preferred to scuttle the ship rather than let her fall into enemy hands.

British diplomats attempted to force Langsdorff to leave or at least have him interned, but he managed to hang on for 72 hours, until 17 December. In the meantime, the British had put out the false intelligence that a huge British force was being assembled, which the Germans had picked up. In fact, there was only *Ajax*, *Achilles* and another ship, *Cumberland*.

Fully convinced that he was facing a greatly superior force, Langsdorff sailed out of the harbour late in the evening of 17 December. Then, watched by thousands of spectators, the ship suddenly and spectacularly exploded. Rather than let *Graf Spee* fall into enemy hands, and thinking there was no hope of escape, Langsdorff had scuttled his ship. Langsdorff and his crew were captured and then taken to Buenos Aires. On 19 December, Langsdorff spread the *Graf Spee*'s ensign on the floor of the room he was being held in, lay down on it and shot himself.

The destruction of the *Graf Spee* was met with predictable jubilation in Britain, but the German High Command, including Hitler, were furious at its loss and the capture of its crew. Admiral Raeder declared that in future: 'The German warship and her crew are to fight with all their strength to the last shell.'

BATTLE OF TARANTO

1940

---

*Pre-emptive attacks on ports had long been a part
of naval warfare and the Japanese attack on Port
Arthur in 1904 showed the effectiveness of torpedo
boats. During World War I ports and naval bases
became ever more defended by nets, mines and guns.
However, the arrival of air power in the twentieth
century gave the navy a new dimension in which
to operate. By the end of World War I, the British
had developed a way of attacking a fleet in its base
by using an aircraft to drop torpedoes. HMS Argus
was commissioned in September 1918 and was
the world's first flat-topped aircraft carrier. Flying
trials began in October, but the war ended before
this system could be thoroughly tested. Between the
wars progress was made in the development of both
aircraft and torpedoes.*

Admiral Sir Andrew Cunningham was in command of the Mediterranean fleet during World War II and used this new tactic to take the fight to the enemy. HMS *Eagle* carried naval air squadrons 813 and 824, which flew the Fairey Swordfish. In July 1940 they sank four Italian destroyers and damaged a fifth. They also sank a submarine, together with two merchant ships, and averted an attack on Alexandria. Cunningham's fleet was augmented at the beginning of September by the new and larger aircraft carrier HMS *Illustrious*. She carried squadrons 815 and 819, also equipped with Fairey Swordfish. On board *Illustrious* was Rear Admiral Lyster, a keen proponent of aircraft equipped with torpedoes. He had previously drawn up a plan to attack the Italian naval base at Taranto during the 1938 Munich crisis. Now, in 1940, this same plan was presented to Cunningham, who greeted it with enthusiasm.

A fire on board *Illustrious* delayed matters and, meanwhile, the Germans invaded Greece, giving added impetus to the need to destroy the Italian fleet. Once the aircraft carrier was repaired, plans were made for the first moonlit night. HMS *Eagle* had suffered some damage and five crews from her squadrons were transferred to *Illustrious* with their aircraft. Part of the plan was for a diversion to be created by the Gibraltar-based carrier HMS *Ark Royal*, which involved bombing Cagliari in Sardinia.

Leaving Alexandria on 6 November 1940, the Mediterranean fleet including *Illustrious* escorted convoys to and from Malta. Meanwhile, intelligence was received from the Royal Air Force about aerial reconnaissance of Taranto. On 11 November, just as it was getting dark, *Illustrious* and four destroyers separated from the fleet and headed to a position 170 miles (274 km) south of Taranto.

Two waves of Swordfish were launched; 12 in the first wave and nine in the second. Led by Lieutenant Commander Williamson, the commanding officer of 815 squadron, six aircraft scored three hits, one on the *Conte di Cavour* and two on *Littorio*. Williamson and his observer, Scarlett, were shot down and taken prisoner. The remainder of that wave dropped bombs on the oil storage depot and divebombed ships in the harbour. In the second wave eight Swordfish reached their targets and scored more hits on the *Latoya*, the *Caio Duilio* and the heavy cruiser *Gorizia*. One aircraft was shot down and its crew were lost.

Between 1 am and 3 am 18 Swordfish returned to *Illustrious*, two of them with minor damage. They knew they had inflicted substantial damage on the Italian battleships and the outer anchorage at Taranto, but had to wait to discover the full details. There were preparations for another strike on the night of 12 November, but with low cloud and rain this was cancelled and the fleet returned to Alexandria.

That afternoon the *Vittorio Veneto*, the *Andrea Doria* and the *Giulio Cesare* sailed for Naples, together with the heavy cruiser and destroyer divisions. This prevented the Italian fleet from being able to react quickly to Allied activity in the central and eastern Mediterranean. The success of the Swordfish crews meant that HMS *Illustrious* became a target for the Luftwaffe and was put out of action in January 1941, forcing the Swordfish to operate from a remote valley in northern Greece. However, the airborne attack on the Italian fleet in its anchorage at Taranto has been described as an example of minimum force 'applied at a critical point and at a critical moment in a campaign'.

BATTLE OF CAPE MATAPAN

1941

The Germans were putting pressure on their Italian allies to disrupt the reinforcement of British forces in Greece. Aware that British convoys were transporting troops from Egypt to Greece, the Italians planned to attack them at Crete and in particular take out what they thought was the one battleship in the theatre. Despite the pummelling it had received at Taranto, the Italian navy still had the very new and fast battleship Vittorio Veneto *and some powerful heavy cruisers. Intelligence was key to the battle of Matapan as was air power, as the Italians had no support from their own air force.*

The commander-in-chief of the British fleet, Admiral Sir Andrew Cunningham, was alerted to the Italians' intentions, while the Italians had underestimated the number of battleships in the eastern Mediterranean. In fact, Cunningham had three battleships and additional air cover. Not only that, but *Formidable* had recently arrived on station to replace the damaged *Illustrious*. Additionally, he could get support from naval aircraft and RAF shore-based units in Crete and Greece to supplement his carrier-based aircraft: Fulmars,

Albacores and Swordfish. Unlike the Italians, the British were experienced in night fighting and also some of their ships had surface warning radar.

Knowing that an attack was imminent, Cunningham suspended convoys and sent out a search force of cruisers and destroyers to the south of Crete, led by Vice Admiral Pridham-Wippell. Cunningham himself sailed from Alexandria after nightfall with his battle fleet to meet Pridham-Wippell's ships. At round 7.30 am on 28 March, crews flying reconnaissance sorties from Crete and from the aircraft carrier *Formidable* saw a fleet of cruisers and destroyers, but could not be certain whether it was the Italians or Pridham-Wippell. It was, in fact, the Italians and Pridham-Wippell then tried to lure them towards the heavy battle force coming from the south. There was a short engagement of about an hour before Admiral Iachino turned his ships away.

Cunningham was now just 70 miles (113 km) from the action and on board *Formidable* there were six torpedo bombers standing ready to attack. After initially pausing to close the gap, Cunningham launched the strike at 9.39 am. The 35,000-ton battleship *Vittorio Veneto* was sailing to the north and Iachino was trying to lure Pridham-Wippell's cruisers towards it. The cruiser HMS *Orion* then sighted the Italian battleship and in the ensuing engagement it was damaged. In this highly dangerous situation Pridham-Wippell was saved by the arrival of the torpedo bombers, which attacked the battleship, forcing the Italians to speed for home. Cunningham, meanwhile, was trying to keep a watch on three groups of enemy ships. The initial attack on the Italian battleship had not done any damage but a second six-aircraft attack in mid-afternoon was more successful, with one torpedo causing severe flooding on the *Vittorio Veneto*. It was able to carry on but at a much slower speed, while the aircraft from *Formidable* were able to give better information, leading to a third aircraft strike.

It did not all go to plan, with communication problems and mistaken identity hampering the operation. The Italians still underestimated the size of the British and Australian ships and had ordered

The Vittorio Veneto. *The Allies' celebrations at Matapan were tempered by the escape of Italy's most dangerous battleship. With typical British understatement, one admiral declared this was something 'much to be regretted'. Fortunately,* Vittorio Veneto *was not able to capitalize on her good fortune, and in 1943 she was surrendered to the Allies. She was scrapped in 1951.*

Vice Admiral Cattaneo to go out with two cruisers, *Zara* and *Fiume*, and four destroyers to assess the situation. They were met by *Formidable*, *Warspite*, *Valiant* and *Barham* and, as Cunningham said, they opened fire at 'at a range even a gunnery officer cannot miss'. *Zara*, *Fiume* and *Vittorio Alfieri* were comprehensively hit and sunk. Cunningham then sent his escorts – the Australian ship *Stuart*, together with *Greyhound*, *Griffin* and *Havock* – to attack and they fought the Italians for two hours.

By dawn British reconnaissance aircraft had assessed the situation. While much of the Italian fleet had been destroyed or damaged, the great battleship *Vittorio Veneto* had escaped. However, no Allied destroyers had been lost and they turned towards Alexandria, fighting off a German bomber attack on the way. The Battle of Cape Matapan had reduced the threat from the Italian fleet and the Axis allies had to turn to air and submarine warfare in the Mediterranean.

THE SINKING OF THE *BISMARCK*

1941

*On 21 May 1941, a reconnaissance aircraft
from the Royal Air Force Coastal Command
photographed two German ships in a Norwegian
fjord. They were the battleship* Bismarck, *then the
most powerful warship afloat, and the* Prinz Eugen,
*a heavy cruiser. Together, these two powerful ships
were a massive threat to the vital convoys that were
keeping Britain in the war. An immediate bombing
attack was ordered and 18 bombers headed
towards Norway, but in very poor visibility only
two of them found the target area and they failed
to do any damage.*

The Royal Navy's commander-in-chief, Admiral Tovey, had two cruisers on patrol between Greenland and Iceland, the *Norfolk* and the *Suffolk*, and other cruisers were between Iceland and the Faroe Islands. He ordered Vice Admiral Holland with his battlecruiser *Hood* and the new battleship *Prince of Wales*, plus their destroyer escorts, to take up position southwest of Iceland. The next day, further reconnaissance confirmed that the two German battleships were no longer in the field. An anxious and urgent search was now on.

The German ships were first sighted by the *Norfolk* and the *Suffolk* in the Denmark Strait between Iceland and Greenland. The *Hood* and the *Prince of Wales* were 300 miles (483 km) away and Admiral Tovey was 600 miles (966 km) away with his battleship *King George V*, the aircraft carrier *Victorious* and the battlecruiser *Repulse*.

Vice Admiral Holland and his two big ships came to within 20 miles (32 km) of the German ships at 5 am on 24 May and in the short action that followed the *Bismarck* succeeded in blowing up and sinking the *Hood*, with the loss of almost all of her 1,400 men. Just three escaped. The *Prince of Wales*, still barely out of the builder's yard and with a new and inexperienced crew, was hit seven times and had to turn away, but the *Bismarck* too had been damaged and had been hit three times by cannon shells, one of which had put the boiler room out of action. Lütjens, *Bismarck*'s commander, decided to head for a port to make repairs and headed south. He was followed by the *Suffolk* and *Norfolk* and the damaged *Prince of Wales*, whose commanders knew that Tovey with the *King George V* and the *Repulse* was approaching from the east. The aircraft carrier *Victorious* was sent to attack the *Bismarck* and nine of her Swordfish aircraft were launched, but they only managed to score one hit on the *Bismarck*.

The *Bismarck* now did everything to lose its pursuers, and on 25 May Tovey received the news that contact had been lost. The Royal Navy had ships converging into the Atlantic from all directions but all of the vessels involved in the chase were running short of fuel. *Bismarck*, damaged and low on fuel, was aiming for the French coast, with just sufficient reserves to reach Brest. On 26 May, the Germans were hopeful that they might succeed but at 10.30 am, when they were just 700 miles (1,127 km) away from their destination, they were seen by a Catalina aircraft. The co-pilot was an American naval ensign, Leonard Smith, who was flying as a special observer since America was not then in the war. North of the *Bismarck* was Vice Admiral Sir James Somerville and his Gibraltar squadron: the *Renown*, *Ark Royal* and *Sheffield*. The *Sheffield* steered for the *Bismarck* to shadow her and 15 torpedo aircraft took off from the *Ark Royal* to attack her. Unaware of the presence in the area of the *Sheffield* they attacked the wrong ship, but fortunately the *Sheffield* was able to evade their torpedoes.

A second wave of torpedo aircraft left the *Ark Royal* at 6.30 pm but signalled that they had been unsuccessful. Then, to general astonishment, a second signal arrived, this time from the *Sheffield*, giving the course of the *Bismarck*. It was steering directly towards the *King George V* and the *Rodney*. The air attack had been successful and one of the two hits had damaged the steering gear of the *Bismarck*, which had jammed the rudders. In vain the Germans dispatched U-boats, bombers and tugs to try to save the crippled ship. The *Rodney* and the *King George V* opened fire on the *Bismarck* from 12 miles (19 km) at 8.45 am on 27 May.

Admiral Tovey described the last moments of the *Bismarck* in a dispatch sent on 5 July 1941.

By 10:15 the Bismarck *was a wreck, without a gun firing, on fire fore and aft and wallowing more heavily every moment. Men could be seen jumping overboard ... I was confident that the* Bismarck *could never get back to harbour and that it was only a matter of hours before she would sink.*

The shortage of fuel oil in the King George V *and the* Rodney *had become acute. I had to consider the possibility of damage to fuel tanks by a near miss by bomb or hit by a torpedo. Further gunfire would do little to hasten the* Bismarck's *end. I therefore decided to break off the action with* King George V *and* Rodney *and I instructed any ship still with torpedoes to use them on the* Bismarck. *The* Dorsetshire *anticipated my order and torpedoed the* Bismarck *at close range on both sides. She sank at 10:37. The* Bismarck *had put up a most gallant fight against impossible odds, worthy of the old days of the Imperial German Navy, and she went down with colours still flying. The* Dorsetshire *picked up four officers, including the third gunnery officer, and 75 ratings, the* Maori *picked up 24 ratings; but at 11:40 the* Dorsetshire *sighted a suspicious object, which might have been a U-boat, and ships were compelled to abandon the work of rescue.*

The German bombers arrived too late and managed to sink just one destroyer, but all the other British ships returned to base. The *Prinz Eugen*, which had previously evaded the pursuers, subsequently slipped into Brest on 1 June.

PEARL HARBOR

1941

*The Japanese attack on the United States Navy in
Pearl Harbor in December 1941 has remained in
the national consciousness as a devastating blow
to the American nation and was the final factor
in bringing the United States into World War II.
Relations between Japan and the United States had
been tense for some time, and when Japan invaded
China in 1937 the United States imposed economic
sanctions on Japan while providing assistance to
China. President Franklin Roosevelt was concerned
about Japanese expansion plans and the Pacific
Fleet remained at its forward base at Pearl Harbor
in Hawaii.*

The US view was that any attacks from the Japanese would be in the Philippines or other nations' possessions and the Pacific. Admiral Yamamoto, who was commander-in-chief of the Japanese navy, had already conceived the plan for an attack on Pearl Harbor, however, and on 26 November he left with 32 ships, including six aircraft carriers. As they headed towards Pearl Harbor diplomatic negotiations were still continuing between the Japanese and the United States.

In a co-ordinated move at 7.55 am the first wave of 183 aircraft attacked the battleships lying at anchor in the harbour and also attacked airfields to prevent retaliation. Shortly after this, in Washington, the Japanese ambassador to the United States delivered a message breaking off diplomatic negotiations, but made no reference to war.

On board the 30,000-ton battleship *Arizona* its air raid siren sounded just before 8.00 am. A solitary Japanese aircraft passed low overhead and then they saw a formation of high-level bombers heading for the battleship. One bomb hit the ship and went through the main deck, exploding on the deck below. Ten minutes later, the forward powder magazines exploded and the order was given to abandon ship. The second wave of 167 aircraft arrived at 8.40 am.

Within one and a half hours 18 ships were sunk or had run aground, including five battleships. There were more than 90 ships in the harbour and the attack concentrated on the eight battleships. USS *West Virginia* sank, as did the *Oklahoma*; USS *California*, *Maryland* and *Tennessee* were damaged. Men fought back as best they could with anti-aircraft fire and attempted with great courage to save the lives of their comrades. In a brief lull, USS *Nevada* managed to get away, but as she moved towards the sea she was stopped by the second wave of Japanese bombers. They tried to sink her in the channel and block the entrance to the harbour, but the *Nevada* managed to beach herself and keep the channel clear. By the end of the assault US losses were 2,403 killed and 1,178 wounded.

Nearly half of the fatalities were due to the explosion of the *Arizona*. Most of those killed were youthful junior enlisted personnel as most of the officers had housing on shore. In all, 187 aircraft, eight battleships, three cruisers, three destroyers, two auxiliary craft and a minelayer were lost. Few aircraft were able to take off to fight back. One saving grace was that the US aircraft carriers were not there at the time and the Japanese omitted to attack repair facilities, submarine pens and fuel storage tanks. In the attack on an unprepared enemy before the official declaration of war Japan lost just 29 aircraft, six submarines and 64 men.

This Japanese pilot's-eye view of the attack on Pearl Harbor shows how the US vessels were sitting ducks in the event of a surprise assault.

The official announcement of the losses from Colonel Frank Knox, US Navy Secretary, on 16 December inevitably made light of the damage but admitted the high number of casualties. He said: 'The entire balance of the Pacific Fleet, with battleships, aircraft carriers, heavy and light cruisers, destroyers, and submarines, are uninjured, and are all at sea seeking contact with the enemy.' Honolulu Harbor facilities, he added, were not damaged, nor were oil tanks or depots destroyed. President Roosevelt made a short speech to a joint session of Congress in which he said: 'Yesterday, December 7th, 1941 – a date which will live in infamy – the United States of America was suddenly and deliberately attacked by naval and air forces of the Empire of Japan.' He finished by requesting Congress to declare war on Japan. Just over 30 minutes later the vote was taken and agreed, supported across the political divide.

A few days later, in another effective aerial attack, the Japanese sank the Royal Navy's new battleship *Prince of Wales* and the battlecruiser *Repulse* off Malaya. This was a major loss for the British and left them without a viable fleet in the Far East. The British prime minister, Winston Churchill, later recalled his feelings when he heard the news:

In all the war, I never received a more direct shock ... As I turned over and twisted in bed the full horror of the news sank in upon me. There were no British or American ships in the Indian Ocean or the Pacific except the American survivors of Pearl Harbor, who were hastening back to California. Across this vast expanse of waters, Japan was supreme, and we everywhere were weak and naked.

At Pearl Harbor all but three of the ships were subsequently raised and repaired. America's highest military award, the Medal of Honor, was awarded to 15 naval personnel of all ranks, ten of them posthumously. The collective shock and the resulting anger at the attack on Pearl Harbor united the American nation in a determination to win the war.

The USS West Virginia and USS Tennessee after the attack. Although West Virginia was sunk at Pearl Harbor, she was re-floated, repaired and, along with the less extensively-damaged Tennessee, went on to see action at Iwo Jima and Leyte Gulf.

BATTLE OF THE JAVA SEA

1942

After the attack on Pearl Harbor and the loss of the British warships Prince of Wales *and* Repulse, *the Japanese navy made landings across the Dutch East Indies, supported by the Japanese Air Force. On the night of 15 February, the British prime minister Winston Churchill announced that Singapore had fallen. It was another link added to the chain of Allied disasters. In his classic style he said, 'Tonight the Japanese are triumphant. They shout their exaltation to the world. We suffer. We are taken aback. We are hard pressed. But I'm sure, even in this dark hour, that criminal madness will be the verdict which history will pronounce upon the authors of Japanese aggression.'*

The remaining Allied naval ships in the area had no air cover and were made up of a mixture of British, Dutch, Australian and American cruisers under the command of an American, Admiral Hart, but the Dutch wanted one of their own, Vice Admiral Helfrich, to take charge. He knew the area very well, having been brought up there, and on 16 February he took command not just of the Allied navies but also of what was left of all three services. This force was known as ABDA, the initials of the four Allies.

At his headquarters in Western Java, Helfrich received air reconnaissance reports of three large Japanese invasion convoys heading towards Java on 25 February. Helfrich's deputy was another Dutchman, Rear Admiral Karel Doorman, who decided to take on the first invasion convoy. Doorman led a group of Allied ships from Surabaya to sea on 26 February in his 6-inch-gunned cruiser, *De Ruyter*. With no aircraft carrier he had no way of getting reconnaissance reports and had limited intelligence from Helfrich's HQ. In his fleet he had two heavy cruisers, HMS *Exeter* and USS *Houston*, with 8-inch (200 mm) guns. *Exeter* had a very experienced crew under the command of Captain Oliver Gordon. There was also an Australian cruiser, HMAS *Perth*, with 6-inch (150 mm) guns and the *Java*, a Dutch vessel also with 6-inch guns. Finally, there were the nine destroyers. HMS *Electra*, *Encounter* and *Jupiter* were British, HNLMS *Kortenaer* and *Witte de With* were Dutch and USS *Alden*, *John D. Edwards*, *John D. Ford* and *Paul Jones* were elderly American destroyers. All of these vessels had been at sea almost continuously for some time and the men and the ships were suffering the effects.

In the afternoon of 27 February they sighted a Japanese cruiser and several destroyers. In total there was an invasion convoy of 41 transports being escorted by 13 destroyers and two light cruisers. Rear Admiral Takeo Takagi also had two heavy cruisers, *Nachi* and *Haguro*. They had a greater firepower, with ten 8-inch guns each and torpedoes. The two Japanese cruisers attacked at 4.00 pm, heading first for the *Exeter* and the *Houston*. Initially Doorman's fleet was able to press forward to attack the convoy, but they were hampered by poor communications between the Allies and bad weather. One hour later a shell exploded in the boiler room of *Exeter*, putting all boilers out of action, and she had to turn back towards Surabaya accompanied by *Witte de With*. HNLMS *Kortenaer* was hit by a Japanese torpedo and sank, HMS *Electra* was damaged and a serious fire meant the ship had to be abandoned. Another ship, *Jupiter*, was sunk by a mine. At nightfall the Allied fleet had broken up, with the destroyers heading back to Surabaya, and Doorman was left with just four cruisers. The *De Ruyter* and *Java* were sunk by torpedoes and only 111 men were saved from both ships. The remaining two ships, HMAS *Perth* and USS *Houston*, retired. Doorman's Eastern Strike Force failed in its unrealistic objective to stop the invasion fleet but it did delay it by a day.

At Surabaya the surviving ships were the *Exeter*, the *Encounter*, the Dutch *Witte de With* and the four American destroyers, plus USS *Pope*, which had not sailed with the strike force due to ongoing repairs. The ships were ordered to leave the area and four American destroyers escaped through the Bali Strait into the Indian Ocean in the darkness of 28 February. The *Witte de With* remained behind, in need of repairs, so the *Exeter*, the *Encounter* and the *Pope* sailed for the Sunda Strait, unable to take the same route as the American destroyers as the water was too shallow for the *Exeter*.

Once into the Java Sea the three vessels were doing well until the early light of the morning, when they were seen by enemy reconnaissance aircraft, and by mid-morning they were surrounded. After fighting until they ran out of ammunition the order was given to abandon ship and the *Exeter* sank. A few minutes later the *Encounter* also went down. The *Pope*'s captain had hoped to escape but she was followed by Japanese bombers and eventually sank on the afternoon of 1 March.

The main ABDA naval force was almost totally destroyed. Ten ships and approximately 2,173 men were lost. The Battles of the Java Sea ended significant Allied naval operations in Southeast Asia. Japan invaded Java and now controlled the whole of the Dutch East Indies, giving them valuable food and oil resources. The last of the Allied forces surrendered in March and the Allied air forces retreated to Australia.

BATTLE OF THE CORAL SEA

1942

*In 1942 Japan strengthened its hold on the East,
controlling large parts of China and taking the
Philippines, Malaya and Rangoon in Burma.
Australia was now under threat and to prove the
point the most northern town in Australia, Darwin,
was bombed in a Japanese raid.*

A complete rethink was required and the British Far East Fleet was now based at Ceylon (Sri Lanka). Aware of the risks, Admiral James Somerville moved his fleet to a deep-water anchorage at Addu Atoll and on 5 April Admiral Nagumo and his fleet, including the aircraft carriers *Akagi* and *Kaga*, prepared to attack Colombo, only to discover the fleet had gone. Thwarted of a repeat of Pearl Harbor, their only success was in destroying two 10,000-ton British cruisers, the *Dorsetshire* and the *Cornwall*, which were on their way to join Somerville's fleet. On the following morning, 1,100 survivors were picked up. The Japanese also found and sank the 11,000-ton *Hermes* on the north coast of Ceylon.

Meanwhile, the Americans were taking a bold step in the fightback. From the advanced American base at Midway Island, two aircraft carriers were dispatched towards Japan. Sixteen long-range bombers took the fight directly to the Japanese mainland and successfully bombed targets in Tokyo and the naval shipyard at Yokohama. After the failure to find the British Eastern Fleet and the mainland attack the Japanese rethought their plans. Their priority now was to consolidate their Pacific bases and their next targets were the islands around the Coral Sea. They moved eastwards to the islands of New Britain, New Ireland, New Guinea and the Solomon Islands. From here they planned to capture the Midway Islands, which would place them in a position to attack Hawaii.

The Americans had highly effective codebreakers and were aware of the Japanese plans, so they sent two carrier groups to the Coral Sea: USS *Lexington*, which could support 60 aircraft, and USS *Yorktown*, plus their supporting cruisers and destroyers. Under the command of Admiral Frank Fletcher they assembled south of Guadalcanal on 5 May and then headed to intercept the Japanese. The Japanese had two groups, the larger of which had two carriers, *Shōkaku* and *Zuikaku*, each of which could carry 84 aircraft. The second group had a smaller carrier, *Shōhō*, and its escorts.

It was *Shōhō* that was found by an advance force of Australian and American cruisers, which successfully and triumphantly dispatched it, losing just three aircraft in the process. The next part of the battle was not so straightforward. The weather was misty and there was some tropical rain as Admiral Fletcher and Admiral Takagi sought each other in poor visibility. On 8 May they were aware of each other's position and both sides scrambled their bombers and fighters from the decks. The Americans were successful in bombing *Shōkaku,* which became ablaze, while the Japanese aircraft targeted the larger Allied carrier, the *Lexington*, and scored two hits, causing it to list. The next wave of dive bombers and torpedo bombers headed for the *Yorktown* which, while hit, still managed to avoid the torpedoes and the gun crew were highly successful as they shot down 26 Japanese aircraft.

As the Japanese pilots returned from their missions the limitations for aircraft at sea were exposed. They were unable to land on the damaged *Shōkaku* aircraft carrier and as a result the *Zuikaku* was

The sinking of USS Lexington at the Battle of the Coral Sea. Originally a battlecruiser, she was converted into an aircraft carrier in 1922, so becoming one of the very first vessels of that type.

overwhelmed. So many aircraft were trying to land that some ran out of fuel and crashed into the sea. The *Shōkaku* managed to return to Japan but the Japanese fleet was unable to finish its plans to establish a forward base.

Lexington and *Yorktown* headed back to Pearl Harbor but on the way a major explosion destroyed the *Lexington* and 200 of the crew were lost and 36 of her aircraft. For the American, Australian and New Zealand Allies the Battle of the Coral Sea was a victory against the larger Japanese force for the loss of one small aircraft carrier. It was the beginning of a hard fightback by the Allies in the Pacific.

BATTLE OF MIDWAY

1942

Until June 1942 the Japanese could still claim a run
of victories, although the Battle of the Coral Sea
in May showed the American cruiser fleet still had
force. It did not, however, stem Japan's aggressive
expansion plans. Admiral Yamamoto, the Japanese
commander-in-chief, was determined to flush out
the Pacific Fleet belonging to the United States.
Japan had received reports that the United States
only had four aircraft carriers compared to the
Japanese Pacific fleet's seven large and four small
aircraft carriers. The Japanese plan was to invade
Midway Island, an American forward base, while
at the same time create a diversion by attacking the
Aleutian Islands, near Alaska.

As he set out flying his flag on the *Yamato*, a new 65,000-ton battleship
with 18-inch (450 mm) guns, Admiral Yamamoto was unaware that
American intelligence already knew the plan as they had partly broken
the Japanese code through intensive intelligence work. As a result,
Admiral Chester Nimitz, the commander-in-chief of the US Pacific
Fleet, was able to position his fleet in readiness north of Midway
Island and maintain reconnaissance patrols.

On paper the numbers were against Nimitz as he had no battleships, while the Japanese had 11. He had two aircraft carriers, the *Hornet* and the *Enterprise*. His third aircraft carrier, *Yorktown*, had been damaged in May so an army of men, 1,400 of them, worked tirelessly at Pearl Harbor to ensure the carrier was ready in 48 hours instead of the predicted 90 days. Even so, the Japanese had eight aircraft carriers carrying 700 aircraft compared with an American total of 300 aircraft. The other numbers were also bad: 13 cruisers against 22; 28 destroyers to fight 65; and 19 submarines versus 21 Japanese submarines.

Ensign Jack Reed was the pilot of a Catalina on patrol on 3 June and he was the first to see the Japanese at 9 am. Although at the time he reported it as the main battle fleet, what he saw was a transport group commanded by Rear Admiral Tanaka. Nine B-17 Flying Fortresses were sent to attack and while they optimistically thought they had made contact, they were unsuccessful. Rear Admiral Fletcher, wisely, did not believe this was the main force and moved his carriers to the southwest to protect Midway. In the north, the Japanese diversionary fleet, under the command of Admiral Hosogaya, sent aircraft from its carrier to attack Dutch Harbor, causing damage to installations.

Nimitz, meanwhile, was informed at 5.30 am on 4 June of the position of the main attack force, spotted by another Catalina pilot. From the Japanese carriers *Akagi*, *Kaga*, *Hiryū* and *Soryū* in Nagumo's First Carrier Strike Force came a wave of 108 aircraft, which included dive bombers, torpedo carriers and fighter planes, the formidable Japanese Zeros. With advance warning from the radar, by 6.00 am all US aircraft were in the air. The Japanese bombers caused considerable damage, while their fighters shot down 15 US aircraft. In total they only lost six of their own aircraft. The US bombers, on the other hand, had attacked the Japanese carriers with little success and considerable loss of aircraft. Seventeen of the 26 defending Marine Corps fighters were lost. It had not been good but the airfield at Midway was still usable.

Fighters preparing to launch from USS Enterprise. The Battle of Midway established beyond all doubt that the future of naval warfare lay with the use of aircraft carriers.

Japanese intelligence learnt of the American carrier movements out of Pearl Harbor and assumed that at least one task force was at sea, but Yamamoto had insisted on strict radio silence and was not given this intelligence. The heavily defended Japanese carriers were attacked first by torpedo bombers from the three American carriers and then the dive bombers from *Enterprise* and *Yorktown* moved in. The fighters and bombers were unable to make their mark and the American losses mounted without seeing any dent in the Japanese fleet. Then 37 dive bombers from USS *Enterprise* came in, led by Lieutenant Commander McCluskey. He separated them into two groups so that half targeted *Kaga* and the other half targeted *Akagi*, at a time when the Japanese fighter planes had not gained sufficient height. Captain Tom Moore, a Marine Air Corps dive bomber, was one of the pilots. He and his rear gunner, private Charles Huber, headed for *Kaga* and *Akagi* and flew through the Japanese fighters to bomb their targets. They were attacked by the Zeros and Huber was hit in the leg. Moore flew his damaged aircraft back with limited fuel and no functioning navigation instruments. He landed back at Midway with just two or three minutes of fuel left.

Akagi was hit three times and soon was ablaze, which caused bombs on board to explode, while *Kaga* was hit four times and the crew had to abandon her. It went down with the loss of 800 men. The third aircraft carrier, *Soryū*, was attacked by dive bombers from the *Yorktown* at a time when there was no fighter cover operating. She too was badly damaged and set on fire and had to be abandoned. The *Hiryū* was to the north and her aircraft headed for *Yorktown* by simply following the returning US aircraft. While ten Japanese aircraft were shot down, six bombers succeeded in seriously damaging the ship, putting its radar and radio out of service and forcing Rear Admiral Fletcher to move his flag to the *Astoria*. A second wave of Japanese torpedo bombers from the *Hiryū* succeeded in hitting *Yorktown* twice and by mid-afternoon the ship had to be abandoned, but all of her crew were rescued.

The *Hiryū* needed to be silenced and four Douglas bombers led by McCluskey flew from the *Enterprise* without fighter escort to tackle the last Japanese carrier, successfully scoring four hits despite the best efforts of the anti-aircraft guns. The *Hiryū* was lost and Admiral Yamamoto, who was still some distance away, realized he had underestimated the number of operational American carriers and called off the operation. If the firepower statistics at the beginning of the battle were overwhelmingly in favour of the Japanese, by the end of the battle mortality rates told another story, as over 3,000 Japanese died compared to just over 300 Americans.

It was an enormous morale boost to the Americans and all the Allies. Newspapers carried the welcome news from Admiral Nimitz on 7 June. Giving some details of the losses, additionally he stated his belief that some of the damaged Japanese vessels would possibly not reach home, but warned 'that vengeance for the Pearl Harbor attack will not be complete until Japanese sea power has been reduced to impotence. We have made substantial progress in that direction. Perhaps we will be forgiven if we claim we are about midway to our objective.'

The Battle of Midway was to be a major turning point in World War II by bringing an abrupt end to Japanese expansion and totally proved that the aircraft carrier, and not the large battleship, was now the major force at sea. Air superiority would now become the critical factor for the rest of the war.

THE BATTLES FOR GUADALCANAL

1942

A small barren island became the focus of the battle for supremacy in the Pacific in the second half of 1942 and sea power was as essential for the Allies as it was for the Japanese. After the Battle of Midway the United States planned an offensive against the Japanese, but there was little agreement among the senior staff about the objectives. However, this was soon settled when intelligence came in indicating the Japanese were occupying areas of the Solomon Islands.

This string of islands was key to Japan's expansion plans, as they intended to use it as their forward base to attack Australia. They had captured a small island called Guadalcanal on which they were creating an airbase. The main Japanese base in the area was at Rabaul on the island of New Britain, now part of Papua New Guinea. They also held the island of Tulagi and part of nearby Florida Island to the north of Guadalcanal. Rabaul, with its magnificent harbour, could be supported from the main Japanese base 640 miles (1,030 km) away at Truk. For Washington, these moves threatened the supply lines from the US to Australia, where General Douglas MacArthur had his base in Brisbane. Here MacArthur was building up Allied forces for the defence of Australia and New Zealand and was planning a counter-offensive to free the Philippines.

Guadalcanal was out of range of Allied land-based fighters, but could be reached by Japanese fighters from the other islands in the Solomons. This made aircraft carriers essential for the Allies as they could provide fighter escorts for long-range land-based bombers. On 7 August 1942 the United States Navy landed 19,000 marines, who were able to overwhelm the Japanese on Guadalcanal. These were largely men working on the airbase, which at the time was little more than a level area on the mountainous island. The marines occupied an area of 15 square miles (39 square km) which included the airstrip, renamed Henderson Field, which could be used as a temporary base for aircraft from the carriers. During the next six months fighting continued almost every day on the island, around the island, at sea and in the air, in a battle to gain control and the use of one airstrip on a small island. The Japanese supplied their forces with convoys from Rabaul by sailing down the channel between the islands. The channel became known as the slot. The Japanese mainly unloaded at night from the transport ships and these convoys became known as the Tokyo Express. It was a long and arduous series of battles between the Japanese navy and the United States Navy, together with the Royal Australian Navy.

Battle of Savo Island

The seizure by US marines of the airbase on Guadalcanal took the Japanese by surprise and they counter-attacked. Admiral Mikawa left Rabaul with three light cruisers and five heavy cruisers on 8 August. Travelling mainly at night, in the early hours of 9 August they saw the Australian heavy cruiser HMAS *Canberra* and USS *Chicago*. Mikawa's squadron opened fire and a torpedo strike killed the captain and all the men on the bridge of the *Canberra* and destroyed the *Chicago*. The heavy cruiser *Vincennes* was also destroyed as was the *Quincy*, but the *Astoria* was more fortunate, although badly damaged. It was a major blow for both the US and the Australian navies. The Allied dead were 1,023 and 709 were wounded. Out of 819 Australian men on the *Canberra* there were 193 casualties, of whom 84 were killed, including Captain Getting.

With dawn, Admiral Mikawa headed rapidly back for Rabaul, but the heavy cruiser *Kako* was sunk by an American submarine, which was small comfort to the Allies for a devastating night. However, the airfield at Guadalcanal was now complete and was an essential airbase supported by fighters from the American aircraft carriers. The Japanese, buoyed up by Mikawa's action, were determined not to repeat the losses of Midway and planned to seize control of the waters around Guadalcanal.

Battle of Eastern Solomons, 23–25 August

Operation Ka aimed to reinforce Japanese ground troops on Guadalcanal and destroy the Allied naval forces. During this engagement all the fighting was done by carrier-based or shore-based aircraft and the opposing naval fleets did not actually see each other. A key Japanese target was the American aircraft carrier *Enterprise* and her battleship escort, *Portland*. The *Enterprise* was hit by the attacking aircraft, which damaged the steering control. However, the Americans had trained hard at damage control and the men on board fixed matters to enable it to make 15 knots of headway. In this battle, the Japanese lost a light carrier and about 90 aircraft compared to about 20 aircraft lost by the Americans and the damage to the *Enterprise*. There was no clear victory for either side, but the Japanese convoy with its supplies of troops and equipment for Guadalcanal was forced to turn back.

Battle of Cape Esperance

On 11 October, a large convoy was sent to reinforce the Japanese ground forces fighting on Guadalcanal. Concurrently, they planned an attack on Henderson Field from a task force of three Japanese heavy cruisers and two destroyers. Rear Admiral Norman Scott had a task force of four cruisers and five destroyers and the two naval groups met just before midnight off Cape Esperance. Scott was successful in forcing the Japanese navy to abandon its plan to bombard the airfield after a Japanese cruiser and a destroyer were sunk and another cruiser was badly damaged. The US also lost a destroyer and a cruiser. However, Scott was unable to prevent the supply convoy from completing its mission.

Battle of Santa Cruz

Still determined to land reinforcements on Guadalcanal, the Japanese needed to remove the Allied fleet from the area. On 24 October, the US carrier force met a Japanese carrier force at the battle of Santa Cruz. Three Japanese carriers and five cruisers were damaged by aircraft from USS *Enterprise* and USS *Hornet*. The *Hornet* was badly damaged in the engagement and had to be sunk and the *Enterprise* was also damaged and had to withdraw, but Japan's hope for a crushing defeat of the Allied navy was unrealized. The Japanese had high aircraft losses, losing almost one hundred, but it was the loss of experienced aircrew that would cause them greater problems. The Americans lost 81 aircraft, but the major advantage from this battle was to reduce the participation of Japanese carrier forces in the campaign. Meanwhile, fierce fighting was continuing between ground forces on the island of Guadalcanal.

Naval Battle of Guadalcanal

On 12 November, a cruiser force under Rear Admiral Callaghan engaged the Imperial Japanese Navy in yet another effort to prevent them from reinforcing Guadalcanal. The Japanese had two battleships, *Hiei* and *Kirishima*, under the command of Vice Admiral Abe. They were well trained in night-fighting, unlike the Americans, who lost heavily. Although greatly outnumbered, Callaghan's cruiser force fought gallantly, often at very close quarters. The Japanese wrecked one battleship and sank three cruisers, including the *Juneau* and several destroyers. On board the flagship, heavy cruiser *San Francisco*, Callaghan and three other senior officers were killed and the navigation officer severely wounded on the bridge. Rear Admiral Norman Scott was also killed when the *Atlanta* was badly damaged. Callaghan and Scott were the two most senior officers killed during the six-month campaign. The *Atlanta* could not be saved despite all efforts, and so the men were ordered to abandon the ship and were taken ashore in a landing craft, while a small demolition party remained to sink the vessel before taking a small boat to head for Guadalcanal.

This was the beginning of three days of battle and again Admirals Mikawa and Tanaka tried at night to get troops through. They succeeded in bombing Henderson Field and getting some troops ashore, despite a battle group led by Admiral Kinkaid which comprised the battleships *Washington* and *South Dakota* plus aircraft carrier *Enterprise*. Vice Admiral Kondō, with his four cruisers and destroyers, met Kinkaid on the night of 14 November and Kondō's battleship *Kirishima* was destroyed by the *Washington* in just seven minutes. Two US light cruisers, four destroyers and 35 aircraft were lost and three destroyers were damaged. However, the Japanese lost two battleships, one heavy cruiser, three destroyers, 11 transports and 64 aircraft. Japan's defeat also ended their final significant attempt to dislodge the Allied forces in the eastern Solomons.

Battle of Tassafaronga

Tassafaronga is on the northern coast of Guadalcanal and once more it was a battle to prevent the Japanese from landing troops in late November. The US had the advantage of surface-search radar, which was still fairly new, and they used it to find the Japanese ships and sink one of their destroyers. The Japanese gained an advantage from their Long Lance torpedoes, which were a formidable weapon, sinking one US cruiser and damaging three more. But they were unable to land their troops on the island, where their forces now were badly

The Japanese battleship Kirishima. Attacked by the better armed USS Washington, Kirishima was struck 26 times by enemy fire. She capsized and sank at 3.30 am on 15 November 1942, having successfully been evacuated.

weakened although still fighting with great ferocity. It was the end of Japan's plans for the island and by the end of December the Japanese Imperial High Command ordered the evacuation of forces in the area.

The Japanese withdrew their forces from the lower Solomon Islands in January and on 11 February 1943 the US Navy reported 'all organised resistance on Guadalcanal has ended. Operations now consist of patrols mopping up scattered enemy units.' It was a turning point in the war against the Japanese and the end of their expansion eastwards. Now they were on the defensive.

BATTLE OF NORTH CAPE

1943

At the end of 1943 the German fleet contained the battleship Tirpitz, *the battlecruiser* Scharnhorst *and a number of cruisers and was under pressure from Hitler to prove its value. The war between Germany and the Soviet Union was not going well and the army needed naval support. The British were running supply convoys to northern Russia. One convoy, PQ-18, managed to deliver 150,000 tons of vital materiel and supplies in September 1942. In December 1943 the commander-in-chief of the German navy, Admiral Doenitz, decided that his Battle Group I would attack the next convoy.*

The Arctic convoys had been temporarily halted in March 1943 by Churchill. The problem was that Admiral Sir Bruce Fraser, commander-in-chief of the British Home Fleet protecting British and European waters, had limited resources. Determined attacks on German ships reduced the threat, however, and by November Fraser felt that the convoys could resume. The first few convoys were successful and passed without incident, but then it was reported that the Germans had seen an eastbound convoy, JW55A, so the British were alerted to the increased risk. Fraser headed out on his flagship, *Duke of York*, and rehearsed his planned tactics with his naval force. Arctic convoy

JW55B left Loch Ewe on 20 December 1943 and in the opposite direction came RA 55A, returning empty after a successful trip.

At this time of year in the Arctic it was dark for most of the day and there was some nervousness and uncertainty in the various German commands about making an attack on the convoy. Admiral Doenitz himself was in Paris and urged them to carry on, despite the very bad weather which some felt would reduce the effectiveness of the German destroyers and limit the Luftwaffe's operations. As was later discovered, the Luftwaffe's reports were vague and inaccurate and they were very slow in communicating with the *Scharnhorst*. In charge of the German fleet was Admiral Bey, who was temporary commander, replacing Admiral Kummetz, who had gone on leave in November.

On Christmas Day, the *Scharnhorst* set sail with 2,000 men and five accompanying destroyers. Bey received a stream of orders at this stage, not all of which were clear, and he left so fast that two minesweepers were unable to clear the way for him. The weather conditions were very poor and keeping company in the severe sea conditions, with high waves and dense snow, was very difficult. In the morning the five destroyers were sent forward to look for the convoy but they lost touch with the *Scharnhorst* and Bey continued northwards on his own. Heading towards the *Scharnhorst* was the British convoy protected by Admiral Fraser's fleet. There were two convoys, each with their own escorts, and a cruiser group under the command of Vice Admiral Burnett comprising *Belfast*, *Norfolk* and *Sheffield*. Accompanying Fraser's battleship was the cruiser *Jamaica* and four destroyers.

On 26 December at 8.34 am Burnett's radar located the *Scharnhorst* just 30 miles (48 km) south of the convoy. The *Sheffield* tried unsuccessfully to illuminate the scene by firing a star shell; so, relying on her radar range, *Norfolk* fired and hit the *Scharnhorst*, damaging its forward radar. Bey decided he would try to do some damage to the convoy and then speed away, but Burnett took a shorter route to

The snow-covered projector of HMS Sheffield, highlighting the extreme weather conditions ships and crew encountered when sailing on arctic convoys.

keep between the German battlecruiser and the convoy, and for the second time *Sheffield* signalled 'enemy in sight'. *Scharnhorst* engaged with Burnett's ships with some success, hitting both the *Norfolk* and the *Sheffield*. On board the *Norfolk* the radar was destroyed and one officer and six ratings were killed. At 12.41 pm Bey took the decision to return to base, signalling to his destroyers to call off the search for the convoy.

Burnett followed and sent regular reports to Fraser so that Fraser would know exactly where to find the *Scharnhorst*, with the result that the *Scharnhorst*, despite being the fastest ship in the area, fell into the trap four hours later. At 5 pm a burst of light lit up the *Scharnhorst* and she became the target for the British ships. The 14-inch (356 mm) guns on the *Duke of York* did considerable damage and fired 52 broadsides, some of them within just 200 yards (183 m) of the German ship. *Scharnhorst* returned fire but caused limited damage to the *Duke of York*, so she tried to escape. Her speed, however, had been fatally cut by damage in the boiler room and two sets of destroyers headed towards her and manoeuvred themselves into position to fire their torpedoes. By 7.01 pm the *Duke of York* and *Jamaica* arrived and resumed their attack. The *Scharnhorst* sank 45 minutes later and there were just 36 survivors out of her crew of 2,000.

The British success was the result of the battle-fleet tactics practised by the Royal Navy. Destroyers and cruisers had been effectively used and there had been excellent gunnery from the *Duke of York*. It was considered an example of superior command and control at every level and stage of the battle. However, it would be the last time a British battleship would fight its own kind.

THE BATTLE OF LEYTE GULF

1944

The Philippine Islands were essential to the expanded Japanese empire. As the islands were positioned between the conquered territory in Southeast Asia and the Japanese homeland, shipping passing by was protected from air and surface attacks. Munitions came from Japan to the frontline in Burma and oil came the other way from Borneo and Sumatra to Japan. If the Allies could take the Philippines this vital supply route would be in peril and gaining control of the Philippines would isolate Japan still further.

After gaining control of Guadalcanal, the forces led by Admiral Nimitz began a strategic offensive and targeted the Marshall, Caroline, and Mariana island groups, where their central position provided numerous bases. From there General MacArthur planned an amphibious assault on the island of Leyte in the centre of the Philippines where the building of airfields would enable allied aircraft to get control of the skies. MacArthur was to be supported by the Seventh Fleet commanded by Admiral Kincaid which also included Australian units. Providing a more distanced support was Admiral Halsey with his Third Fleet. There was however no overall commander as Kincaid reported to MacArthur and Halsey's orders came via Admiral Nimitz based in Pearl Harbor.

MacArthur successfully landed on 20 October and announced his intention to liberate the islands. The Japanese initiated their battle plan which involved three separate fleets, Admiral Ozawa to attack from north, Admiral Kurita from west via the San Bernardino Strait and Admirals Shima and Nishimura from southwest. Similarly, they were without an overall commander. Admiral Yamamoto was killed the previous year in an intelligence led attack as he flew back to his headquarters in Papua New Guinea.

Air power was crucial to the operation and the Americans had the advantage of new Grumman Hellcats, fast and well armed. The Japanese pilots were ill trained and short of fuel and aircraft while the US had plenty of both. US pilots also had the knowledge of an excellent air sea rescue service and good safety equipment in well equipped auto inflating rafts and inflatable life jackets.

The US submarines, *Dace* and *Darter*, shadowed Kurita's force and on 23 October they attacked sinking the two cruisers *Atago* and *Maya* and badly damaging his flag ship *Takao*, forcing Kurita to transfer to one of the two massive battleships, *Yamato*. Alerted to Kurita's position in the Sibuyan Sea, Halsey with his carrier force went on the attack at about 8.30 a.m. on the 24 October. It was a long day as scores of US aircraft repeatedly attacked, focusing particularly on the enormous battleship, *Musashi*, which went down at 3.30 pm. A big loss for the Allies came when a lone Japanese aircraft found its way through the defence to drop one 550-pound bomb in the centre of *Princeton*'s flight deck. Fire spread rapidly and despite valiant efforts to save her the ship was abandoned.

Thinking that Kurita's force was no longer a serious menace Halsey headed north to tackle Ozawa who had moved down from the Inland Sea to lure Halsey away. Halsey's decision to leave his position guarding the San Bernardino Strait was controversial and was not helped by communications confusion when Kincaid did not receive all the necessary information. Halsey, however, successfully destroyed Admiral Ozawa's carriers.

But the Japanese were not finished and Rear Admiral Sprague, who only had escort carriers and destroyers and not battleships, faced a shock when Kurita's remaining fleet appeared. It became an unequal destroyer/battleship dual. The *Johnston* and the *Gambia Bay* sank under enemy bombardment and the odds were against the rest of the American destroyers. Suddenly, on the mistaken impression that Sprague's fleet was more substantial than it was, Kurita turned and headed back down the San Bernardino Strait.

If the Japanese battleships had gone the Japanese Air Force was still active, the dive bombers in particular. At 7.25 am on 25 October, a 23-year old pilot named Yukio Seki led his unit of nine Zeros on a special mission. To the horror of those watching, the dive bombers did not pull out of their dive but just kept straight on. Seki flew into the deck of the USS *St Lo*, an American escort carrier. More than 100 men on the ship were killed and Seki made history as the first kamikaze and leader of the first dedicated kamikaze unit.

The battle for the Philippines was a combined force of battleships, submarines and aircraft. Huge numbers were involved, more ships participated than at Jutland, and it was the last great battleship fight. It was also the first-time the desperate kamikaze tactic was employed. The battle lasted four days and was fought over an enormous sea area. It heralded the end of the Japanese navy and was a deciding factor in finishing the war in the Pacific.

THE FALKLANDS WAR

1982

The Falkland Islands are a self-governing British dependency and include the islands of South Georgia and the South Sandwich Islands. By 1982, the population was about 2,000 and was dependent upon its export of wool. South Georgia, once a whaling station, was mainly used for Antarctic scientific work. In 1981, the Argentine military junta launched a diplomatic offensive, claiming sovereignty of the Malvinas, their name for the Falkland Islands, mainly to distract from internal economic problems. The Falkland Islanders were strongly opposed to the idea and the British government had to support them against Argentina.

As part of an overall defence review led by John Nott, Prime Minister Margaret Thatcher's defence minister, HMS *Endurance*, an ice patrol vessel in the South Atlantic, was withdrawn. This removal of the only Royal Navy vessel in the area looked like an open invitation to the Argentine junta to seize the islands. In March 1982, suspicions were raised in London when a party of Argentinians landed in South Georgia saying that they were there to recover scrap from derelict whaling installations. The orders for the Argentine invasion of the Falkland Islands were given on 26 March, and between 1 and 2

April 150 commandos were landed by helicopter from the destroyer *Santísima Trinidad*. A further 600 troops were then landed and the garrison of 81 Royal Marines surrendered after being overwhelmed. On 4 April Argentine forces seized South Georgia.

This caused a political crisis in Britain and left many Britons searching for an atlas in order to discover the location of the islands. Such an insult to Britain's sovereignty required a rapid reply and the first warships left from Portsmouth on 5 April for the South Atlantic. Transport and supply were major issues as the Royal Navy had little in the way of suitable vessels. Merchant ships were adapted with helicopter flight decks and facilities for refuelling at sea, the passenger liner *Canberra* was converted to carry 2,200 troops and container vessels would act as aircraft transports. Cunard's *QE2* was also tasked with carrying troops. Taskforce 317 comprised the aircraft carriers and amphibious forces and its flagship was HMS *Hermes*, refitted to operate Sea Harriers. HMS *Invincible* accompanied her. There were two amphibious ships, *Fearless* and *Intrepid*, and Royal Fleet Auxiliary manned landing ships. Taskforce 324 comprised six submarines, including HMS *Conqueror* and HMS *Courageous*. The *Uganda*, a 1952 steamship which ran educational cruises for P&O, was requisitioned as a hospital ship and refitted at Gibraltar, and was supported by three refitted survey vessels, HMS *Hecla*, HMS *Hydra* and HMS *Herald*, which were to be ambulance ships. At Portsmouth the *Uganda* embarked 136 medical staff, comprising doctors, operating theatre staff and nurses plus medical supplies.

Britain declared an exclusion zone of 200 miles (322 km) in radius around the islands within which 'Argentinian ships and aircraft would be attacked'. The Falkland Islands were 4,000 miles (6,437 km) from Britain and there were many risks in fighting a war at such a distance. There was also an awareness that matters needed to be decided before winter approached.

Helicopters were of particular use in the campaign. Royal Marines were landed on South Georgia on 20 April by helicopter and succeeded in retaking the island, the first success of the campaign. Rather longer distance flying, which required air-to-air refuelling, was undertaken by an RAF Vulcan on 1 May, which bombed Port Stanley Airport. The airport was bombed again by Sea Harriers from *Hermes* and *Invincible* as they arrived to take up station.

On 2 May the *General Belgrano*, an old gun-armed 10,650-ton cruiser, was dispatched rapidly and efficiently by the British submarine HMS *Conqueror* and 321 of the 1,200 people on board were lost, the largest single loss of the conflict. The sinking was controversial as the *General Belgrano* was just outside the exclusion zone, although it was later agreed by the Argentinian government to be a legitimate act of war. This act enabled the British to maintain control of the waters since, in an earlier incident, a helicopter located the Argentinian submarine *Santa Fe* and hit it with its guided missile. The *Santa Fe* managed to ground but its crew had to surrender.

The big threat from Argentina now came from its French-built and supplied Super Etendard aircraft equipped with Exocet missiles, and their first success was to sink the destroyer *Sheffield*, with the loss of 20 of her crew. The hospital ship *Uganda* received her first casualties on 12 May from the *Sheffield* and continued to take both British and Argentinian casualties. The converted survey ships transferred those well enough to Montevideo. Soon she would be even busier as the British forces prepared to take back the islands. Meanwhile, the Argentines managed to fly in additional troops and materiel to Port Stanley Airport during the campaign. A limited number of their naval forces were still operating and they had two submarines, the *Salta* and *San Luis*, but operational difficulties meant they were unsuccessful and ineffective.

On 21 May, a fleet of British ships sailed into the waters between the Western and Eastern Falkland Islands and at San Carlos, 86 miles (138 km) from Stanley, 3,000 men, artillery and supplies were landed. The Argentinian commander had done little to defend that end of the island, thinking it an unlikely place for a landing. However, the defending

Sea King helicopters operating in the Falklands. These versatile aircraft were used to deploy Royal Marines into strategic locations in the Falkland Islands and to rescue downed air crews.

warships protecting the landing were attacked by 72 Argentinian Skyhawk and Mirage jets, frequently operating at the limits of their range. HMS *Ardent* was sunk and *Argonaut* was damaged, but some Argentine aircraft were forced to fly too low for the conventionally fused bombs to explode and several ships were hit by unexploded bombs. On 25 May, *Coventry* was hit, caught fire and sank. Due to the difficult terrain helicopters were vital to carry equipment to assist a fast advance but there came a major setback when the container vessel *Atlantic Conveyor* was hit by an Exocet missile, destroying her cargo of helicopters, Harriers and materiel for a forward operating base. The next day the British Army and the Royal Marines took the decision to continue with the land advance and would carry what they could on foot. Settlements at Darwin and Goose Green were secured from the Argentinian garrison after a hard-fought battle. By 31 May, the *Uganda*, now anchored in Grantham Sound, 11 miles (18 km) northwest of Goose Green, was receiving casualties from both sides by helicopter and now had 132 casualties aboard.

In the Falklands campaign naval gunfire support, which conventional military wisdom considered outmoded in favour of missiles and air combat, came into its own again, providing bombardment and cover from the ships. It restricted the movement of Argentine troops and destroyed or damaged specific targets such as artillery, munitions, radar and bunkers. Used effectively at night it had a demoralizing effect on Argentine troops while it boosted the morale of British troops.

Captain Chris Brown, a naval gunfire forward observer recalled: 'It was very, very obvious to, I think, both friendly forces and to the enemy that they were being either, in the case of friendly forces supported and in the case of the enemy engaged by naval gunfire support and I say that because of this regular clockwork frequency of firing.'

Indeed, during a post-operation briefing, the *Glamorgan*'s crew was told that: '*Glamorgan* was very popular with the troops ashore. Our salvos always landed where and when they were wanted. British troops were quite happy to call down fire from *Glamorgan* a bare 150 yards away.'

A major blow to the advance was the disaster at Bluff Cove south of Port Stanley on 8 June, as the British attempted to surround the capital. The Regiment of Welsh Guards was about to be landed from two Royal Fleet Auxiliary vessels, *Sir Tristram* and *Sir Galahad*. They were seen by Argentinian land forces who called in air support and a wave of Argentinian aircraft hit both ships. Fifty-six troops were killed and many were badly injured. The *Sir Galahad* was scuttled.

On 12 June *Glamorgan*, which was providing naval gun support, was hit by an Exocet missile operated from the land with the loss of 14 men. At San Carlos, an airbase had been established to enable RAF Harriers to provide support for the troops now gathering near Stanley. After a fierce battle for the high ground of Mount Tumbledown the path was open to the port and on 14 June the Argentinian commander at Stanley, General Menendez, surrendered to Major General Jeremy Moore.

The Falklands War was a close-run campaign and engaging a determined enemy so far from home had serious implications. During the 74 days of the conflict 255 British servicemen were killed and three women who were local residents also died. The Argentinians lost 649 men in total. The Royal Navy and the Royal Marines achieved a magnificent feat of arms, proving the value of their services and their global reach, but victory was seriously threatened as air superiority was never achieved, showing the limits of carrier-borne aircraft against an enemy that had land bases.

GLOSSARY

Aftercastle – *see* castle

Aircraft carrier – *see* carrier

Auxiliary steam – having a steam engine as back up to sails

Battle fleet – *see* fleet

Battlecruiser – *see* cruiser

Blockade – a patrol maintained off an enemy port to prevent ships entering or leaving

Bomb vessel – warship fitted to fire heavy mortars for shore bombardment (17th–19th century)

Breaking the line – sailing a right angles through the enemy's line of ships

Brig – a vessel square rigged on two masts

Broadside – the simultaneous firing of guns mounted on one side of a ship

Carrier, Aircraft – a warship fitted to carry aircraft with a flight deck capable of flying off and landing aircraft

Carronade – a type of short iron gun

Castle – a structure erected forward or aft, or on a mast, to provide a fighting platform (12th–15th century)

Cog – merchant ship with a flat bottom, single mast and sail (13th–15th century)

Colours – the national flag or ensign

Commerce raider – an armed ship targeting merchant vessels belonging to an enemy

Convoy – a body of merchant ships under escort

Corvette – a type of small escort vessel

Cruiser – one of several types of warship design for cruising (20th century): armoured cruiser, a large cruiser with extensive vertical armour (19th–20th century); battlecruiser, a type of dreadnought with higher speed and less armour than a battleship

Destroyer, torpedo boat destroyer – a large type of torpedo boat armed with boat torpedoes and guns

Draught – depth of water required to float a ship

Dreadnought – a class of battleship following HMS *Dreadnought* of 1906 with a main armament of heavy guns of one type

East Indiaman – large, heavily-built merchant sailing ship used in trade with Far East

Fireship – vessel filled with combustibles intended to be sent on fire towards the enemy

Flagship – admiral's ship flying his flag

Flat top – nickname for aircraft carriers

Fleet – a large body of ships or warships in company

Flota – Spanish fleet; the annual convoy from West Indies carrying silver from South American mines

Forecastle – *see* castle

Frigate – small warship used as a convoy escort (20th century)

Galleass – a large galley with a full sailing rig and a light gundeck above rowers (16th century)

Galley – warship propelled by oars

General Chase – the pursuit of a flying foe by the victors without regard to order

Guerre du course – French term for privateering

Impressment – recruiting of men, often by force

Ironclad – a warship protected by armour (19th century)

Leeward – relating to the direction towards which the wind is blowing

Line abreast – sailing parallel to another ships

Line astern – sailing behind another ship

Line of battle – a fighting formation in which the ships followed one another in line ahead in predetermined order

Luff – to turn into the wind

Magazine – compartment on a ship for storing for explosives

Man-of-war – warship

Melee – a disorganized fight at close quarters

Mine – a submerged explosive charge designed to sink passing ships

Muster – a record of names of the ship's company

Privateer – merchant vessel licensed to attack ships of a named enemy in war, or an individual on a privateer ship

Prize – a captured vessel which could be sold for prize money

Raking – to fire down the length of an enemy ship from ahead or astern

Rigging – the ropes supporting the mass and spars

Schooner – two-masted fore- and aft-rigged vessel originally native to North America

Shell – an explosive projectile; a star shell is a type of shell exploding as a flare to illuminate at night

Siege train – a device to break down heavy doors, fortifications or walls

Squadron – a group of warships operating under a single command; a division of a fleet

Transport – a merchantman chartered to freight troops or stores; a ship specifically for transporting troops or stores

Trebuchet – a type of massive catapult to hurl projectiles

U-boat – submarine

Van – the leading division of the three divisions of a fleet

Weather gage – the windward position in relation to another ship or fleet

Windward – relating to the direction from which the wind is blowing

INDEX

PICTURE CREDITS